THREE POSITIONS

Surfing Life, Business, and Civilization

I0143136

By
ButterflyMan

Copyright © 2025 by **ButterflyMan Publishing LLC**

All rights reserved.

No part of this book may be reproduced, distributed, or transmitted in any form or by any means, including photocopying, recording, or other electronic or mechanical methods, without the prior written permission of the publisher, except in the case of brief quotations embodied in critical reviews and certain noncommercial uses permitted by copyright law.

For permission requests, contact:
ButterflyMan Publishing LLC
Email: contact@butterflyman.com
Website: www.butterflyman.com

This book is a work of nonfiction.
All concepts, interpretations, metaphors, and frameworks presented herein are the author's own.

First Edition — 2025
Printed in the United States of America

ISBN: 979-8-90217-010-5

Book Design: ButterflyMan Publishing LLC

Table of Contents

Preface

Surfing the Three Positions: From Conflict to Harmony in Life, Business, and Society

Conflict surrounds us. In families, arguments flare over words spoken in anger. In workplaces, projects stall because teams cannot agree. In politics, nations fracture into rival camps, each convinced it alone sees the truth.

Why does this happen so easily? The answer is deceptively simple: **we see the world only from our own position.**

When we stand only in our own shoes, everything looks reasonable. Every excuse seems justified. Every demand feels fair. We ask for favors from others without considering their circumstances. We defend ourselves fiercely, blind to the wider facts. This is human instinct — but it is also the root of nearly every conflict in life, business, and society.

The Trap of One Position

When we remain locked in **our own position**, we fall into illusion. We confuse our perception with reality. We become self-centered, and emotion blinds us to truth. The result: anger at home, failed deals in business, polarization in politics.

A New Framework: Three Positions

To break the trap, we must learn to move beyond one fixed view. This book introduces a practical framework:

1. **Your Position** — the place of ego and self-interest.
   - Necessary, but dangerous if it becomes the only lens.

2. **Neutral Position** — the place of facts and truth.
   - The grounding of reality, the role of serious media, auditors, judges, and mediators.

3. **Opposite Position** — the place of empathy and hidden truth.

- The ability to see through the eyes of your opponent, your critic, or your competitor.

Together, these form a triangle of perspectives. The art is not simply to know them, but to **surf among them**. Like a surfer riding waves, we must learn when to stand firm, when to balance in the middle, and when to dive into the opposite.

Surfing as a Way of Life

Surfing the three positions is not weakness. It is not surrender. It is strength.

- In **life**, surfing helps us avoid unnecessary quarrels and heal relationships with dignity.

- In **business**, it reveals opportunities hidden behind client demands, market shifts, and even competitor strategies. Amazon, Toyota, and Tesla all succeeded by surfing perspectives.

- In **society**, surfing allows peaceful transformation. Chile, Taiwan, and Poland found democracy not by crushing opponents, but by including them.

Surfing the positions prepares us for reality. It makes us adaptable. It allows us to see further than ego alone will ever let us.

The Wisdom of Common Ground

The final wisdom of this book is simple yet profound: **conflicts end only when common ground is found**.

Too often, we wait until after years of suffering to forgive enemies. But what if we considered the opposition at the very beginning? What if empathy came first, not last?

This does not mean abandoning our rights or bending to authority. On the contrary — it means calming our anger so we can fight smarter, negotiate stronger, and transform deeper. It means finding peace without losing dignity.

An Invitation

This book is not philosophy for shelves. It is a tool for everyday life. It will show you:
- How to shift perspectives in family disputes.
- How to surf positions in business strategy.
- How to correct political discourse and move toward social harmony.

It is a practice of balance. A discipline of awareness. A path to wisdom.

Conflict will never disappear. But if you learn to surf the three positions, you will discover that even the strongest waves can carry you forward — toward peace, innovation, and transformation.

Table of content

Chapter 1

Your Position — The Trap of the Self

1. The Illusion of Being Right

Every human being carries a silent conviction: *"I am right."*

This conviction hides in the background of daily life. It appears in small irritations — when a driver cuts us off, when a spouse forgets to do the dishes, when a colleague interrupts in a meeting. It also explodes in large disputes — political campaigns, labor strikes, international conflicts.

The feeling is always the same: *"I see clearly. They do not."*

This is the first trap of life: the **illusion of being right**.

We rarely notice it because it feels so natural. From inside our own minds, our reasons are convincing. Our experiences are valid. Our logic feels airtight. And because of that, it is easy to mistake **our perception for objective truth**.

But perception is not fact. "Seeing is believing," people say. Yet in reality, it is usually **believing first, and then only seeing what fits**.

2. The Structure of the Trap

The trap of Your Position works through three mechanisms:
1. **Self-Centered Reasoning**
    - We filter evidence to support ourselves.
    - We amplify the details that confirm us and silence those that challenge us.
    - This leads to a distorted form of logic where every road leads back to "I am right."
2. **Emotional Amplification**
    - Emotions attach to our position like fire to dry wood.
    - Anger sharpens our words, pride stiffens our back, fear makes us defensive.

- Once emotions rise, reason serves them instead of guiding them.
3. **Distorted Reality**
   - Feelings become facts in our language.
   - "I feel ignored" transforms into "You never listen."
   - "Our country is criticized" becomes "The whole world is against us."
   - The line between perception and reality blurs until we cannot separate them.

This trap exists not because we are evil or foolish, but because we are human. It is the default condition of consciousness.

3. Family: The Small Scale of the Trap

Families are often where the trap shows itself most clearly.

A husband comes home tired and wants quiet. His wife, also exhausted, wants help with the children. The argument begins:

- Husband: *"I've worked all day. Don't you see how tired I am?"*
- Wife: *"I've worked all day too. Why should I carry this alone?"*

Each side is correct in their own position. Each has reasons, each has evidence. Yet neither recognizes that both truths can exist simultaneously.

The result is escalation. Words sharpen. Old resentments reappear. By night's end, they are not arguing about children at all — they are arguing about love, respect, and the fear of being unseen.

The trap of Your Position turns small facts into emotional weapons. In families, it corrodes trust. Left unchecked, it destroys intimacy.

Case Reflection:
- Ask yourself: In my last family conflict, was I defending truth — or just defending *my truth*?

4. Business: When Money Magnifies the Trap

In business, the trap is magnified by money, status, and survival.

A supplier demands higher prices, citing rising costs. A retailer refuses, pointing to market competition. Both sides lock into their own data sets, their own sense of urgency. Meetings drag, deadlines slip, partnerships collapse.

The deeper truth is that each side sees only its own survival:
- The supplier fears bankruptcy.
- The retailer fears losing customers.

Neither considers the whole system. Neither stands in the other's shoes. Each assumes their position is the "real" reality.

Historical Example — Kodak
Kodak once dominated photography. Its executives clung to *their position*: film would always rule. Even when digital photography emerged — and even though Kodak itself invented the digital camera — executives could not abandon their view. They believed their position *was* the market truth.

The result: bankruptcy. Their refusal to see beyond their own lens trapped them.

Lesson: Business failure often begins not with lack of resources, but with blindness to perspectives outside one's own.

5. Politics: The Trap at National Scale

When entire nations fall into Your Position, the consequences are devastating.
- In authoritarian regimes, the ruling party insists: *"We are the only voice of the people."*
- In polarized democracies, each side insists: *"We alone stand for truth, the other side is corrupt."*
- Propaganda reinforces the illusion, building echo chambers where each camp hears only itself.

The result is paralysis or oppression. Compromise becomes betrayal. Neutral institutions like courts or journalists are accused of bias. Citizens lose the ability to talk across differences.

Example — The Cold War

For decades, the United States and the Soviet Union saw themselves as righteous and the other as evil. Each side weaponized ideology. Each saw its system as the only truth. The refusal to acknowledge validity in the opposite view nearly destroyed the world in the Cuban Missile Crisis.

Only when leaders briefly stepped beyond their own position — Kennedy acknowledging Soviet fears, Khrushchev acknowledging American resolve — was nuclear war avoided.

Lesson: At national scale, the trap of Your Position can threaten humanity itself.

6. Why We Cling to the Trap

The persistence of this trap comes from deep roots:
- **Identity Protection**: Opinions feel like part of the self. To question them feels like questioning existence.
- **Fear of Weakness**: Cultures teach that compromise is weakness. "Stand your ground," we are told, even if ground becomes a prison.
- **Short-Term Satisfaction**: Defending ourselves feels good. Anger provides relief, pride provides power — even if only briefly.
- **Cultural Conditioning**: In hierarchical societies, authority demands obedience. People learn to cling to assigned positions rather than question them.

Together, these roots form a cage that most people never notice.

7. The Hidden Cost

The cost of staying trapped in Your Position is immense:

- **Families** collapse into resentment, cold silence, divorce.
- **Businesses** miss innovation, ruin partnerships, stagnate.
- **Societies** drift toward violence, suppression, even war.

The cost is not only external. It is internal: **anger, stress, loneliness.** The more we cling to our position, the more isolated we become.

8. A Glimpse of Escape

Yet the trap is not permanent. A glimpse of freedom appears when we pause to ask:
- *"What are the facts beyond my feeling?"*
- *"What might the other side fear?"*
- *"Is my anger creating truth, or hiding it?"*

Even a small shift cracks the walls. For one moment, we see that our position is not the whole universe. That recognition is the first step toward surfing.

9. Expanded Case Studies

Family Story — A Father and Son

A teenage son refuses to study. The father insists: *"If you don't study, your future is ruined."* The son replies: *"It's my life, stop controlling me."*

Both cling to their position. The father sees himself as protective, the son sees himself as oppressed. Weeks of shouting pass, until silence replaces words.

The truth: both fear failure. The father fears his son's future, the son fears living without freedom. The common ground — fear — is invisible until one side steps beyond their own position.

Business Story — Amazon

Jeff Bezos insisted on customer obsession. Many employees resisted, insisting: *"We already provide good service, why push harder?"* Bezos refused to stay in the employee's position or the supplier's position. He forced himself into the **customer's opposite position** — what would customers demand if they had no loyalty? That surfing created Amazon Prime, logistics dominance, and one of the largest companies in history.

Political Story — Poland

In the 1980s, Poland faced dictatorship and economic collapse. Workers struck, the government threatened force. Instead of only defending their own position, leaders found neutral mediators (the Catholic Church) and considered the opposite's fear (collapse into chaos). The result: roundtable talks, elections, and peaceful transition.

10. Exercises for Readers

1. **Conflict Journal**

   - Recall your last argument.
   - Write your position in detail.
   - Write what facts you ignored.
   - Write what the other side might have feared.
   - Imagine the outcome if you had acknowledged those fears.

2. **Three-Minute Pause**

   - Next time anger rises, pause for 3 minutes before speaking.
   - In that silence, ask: *"Am I defending truth, or just myself?"*

3. **Perspective Drill**

   - Take a news article you disagree with.
   - Write a paragraph defending it as if it were your own view.
   - Notice what truths you had ignored before.

11. Closing Thought

Your Position is not the enemy. It is your anchor, your voice, your starting point. But when you mistake it for the whole truth, it becomes a prison.

The first wisdom is recognition: *"I may not be wrong, but I am not the whole."*

From here, the door opens — to Neutral Position, to Opposite Position, to the art of surfing them. The journey of this book begins with this single awareness: **your reasons are not the universe, and your emotions are not facts.**

Chapter 2

Neutral Position — The Ground of Facts

1. Why Neutrality Matters

If **Your Position** is the home of ego and emotion, then **Neutral Position** is the ground of reality.

The Neutral Position does not ask, *"What do I feel?"* or *"What do I want?"* It asks: *"What are the facts?"*

In a world where information is twisted by bias, propaganda, and self-interest, neutrality is the rarest and most valuable resource. Families fight because emotion drowns out truth. Businesses fail because leaders mistake opinions for data. Nations collapse when propaganda silences independent institutions.

Neutral Position is not about indifference. It is not "both-sides-ism." It is not silence. It is an **active search for truth beyond personal bias**.

2. What Neutral Position Is (and Isn't)

Neutral is:
- A stance of curiosity, not judgment.
- Grounded in evidence, data, and observable facts.
- The position journalists, auditors, scientists, and judges *should* take.

Neutral is not:
- Weakness.
- Avoidance of conflict.
- Pretending that both sides are equal when one side clearly distorts truth.

True neutrality is like standing on solid ground in the middle of a storm. The winds of Your Position and Opposite Position blow fiercely. Neutrality anchors you, so you do not get carried away.

3. Family: Neutrality as a Healer

In family conflict, neutrality means refusing to fight only from ego.

A father shouts at his teenage daughter for staying out late. His position: *"You are irresponsible."*
The daughter shouts back: *"You don't trust me!"*

Both are trapped in their positions. Anger builds. Trust erodes.

Now imagine a grandmother in the room, calm and neutral. She does not shout. She asks:

- *"What time did you come home?"*
- *"Did you tell anyone where you were going?"*
- *"What rules were agreed upon in the past?"*

By grounding the argument in **facts**, not feelings, she creates space for resolution. Maybe the daughter was late, but only by 30 minutes. Maybe the father's fear is valid, but his assumption exaggerated. Neutrality dissolves distortion.

Families need such neutral voices. Without them, arguments become endless battles of emotion.

4. Business: Neutral as Competitive Advantage

In business, neutrality means replacing assumption with measurement.

A CEO believes customers love the company's product. He feels confident. His position: *"We are market leaders."*

But neutral data tells a different story. Surveys show falling satisfaction. Sales data shows rising churn. Competitors are innovating faster.

If the CEO refuses neutral facts, the company collapses. If he embraces them, transformation is possible.

Case Study — Netflix

In the early 2000s, Netflix mailed DVDs. Its position: *"People love renting by mail."* But neutral data revealed a shift: broadband internet was spreading, and customers wanted instant streaming. Blockbuster ignored facts, clinging to its position. Netflix listened to neutrality. The result: a global transformation of entertainment.

Lesson: Neutral Position sees what ego ignores. It transforms markets.

5. Politics: Neutrality as Democracy's Shield

At a societal level, Neutral Position is embodied in **institutions**:
- Independent courts.
- Free press.
- Non-partisan auditors and fact-checkers.
- Transparent science.

When societies lose neutral ground, discourse collapses. Citizens live in echo chambers. Each camp insists it has "truth." Without a neutral referee, conflict escalates into violence.

Example — Taiwan's Transition

During its democratic transition, Taiwan established neutral institutions: election commissions, independent media, constitutional courts. These bodies anchored facts in the storm of political rivalry. Neutrality protected democracy from sliding into chaos.

Counter-Example — Authoritarian Regimes

In authoritarian states, neutrality is destroyed. Courts serve the party. Media spreads propaganda. Facts are replaced by "narratives." Once neutrality dies, truth itself dies — and only power remains.

6. The Obstacles to Neutrality

Neutrality is rare because it is difficult. Three forces resist it:

1. **Ego Pull**

   • Our emotions demand that our side be right. Neutrality feels like betrayal.

2. **Cultural Conditioning**

   • Many societies reward loyalty to tribe, party, or family. Neutrality is punished as weakness.

3. **Manipulation**

   • Propaganda machines deliberately attack neutrality. They say: "You are either with us or against us."

Neutrality requires courage. It requires resisting the gravitational pull of ego, tribe, and manipulation.

7. Cultivating the Neutral Mind

How can individuals practice Neutral Position?

- **Pause and Check**: Before reacting, ask: *"What are the actual facts?"*
- **Seek Sources**: In disputes, look for independent evidence.
- **Ask Clarifying Questions**: Instead of defending yourself, ask: *"What exactly happened?"*
- **Separate Feeling from Fact**: Say, "I feel ignored," instead of "You never listen."

These practices are simple but revolutionary. They transform shouting matches into grounded dialogue.

7.   Exercises for Readers

1.   The Fact Filter

- Recall your last argument.
- Write down only the verifiable facts (times, dates, actions).
- Cross out emotional language.
- Notice how small the actual facts are compared to your feelings.

2.   Neutral News Drill

- Take one political issue.
- Read coverage from three different sources.
- Extract only the facts, leaving opinions aside.
- Notice how the facts remain stable, but interpretations differ.

3.   The Mirror Question

- In a conflict, ask yourself: *"If I were a neutral judge, how would I describe this situation?"*

9. The Paradox of Neutrality

Neutral Position does not mean abandoning values. It does not mean silence in the face of injustice. It means clarity before action.

- Neutrality clarifies whether your anger is justified.
- Neutrality prevents manipulation by false narratives.
- Neutrality allows fair judgment, even when you must still take a side.

In fact, true strength comes from standing firmly in Your Position **after** passing through Neutral Position. When your stance is tested against facts, it gains legitimacy.

10. Closing Thought

Neutrality is the ground of truth. It is the middle anchor between ego and empathy. Without it, families break, businesses collapse, and societies descend into propaganda and violence.

But with it, conflict becomes manageable. Decisions become wiser. Transformation becomes possible.

👉 To surf the three positions, you must learn to stand here — calmly, clearly, courageously — on the ground of facts.

Chapter 3

Opposite Position — The Door to Empathy

1. Why Step Into Opposition?

Conflict locks us into a simple reflex: defend ourselves, attack the other.

When your spouse criticizes you, your instinct is to explain or counterattack. When a client rejects your proposal, you defend your design. When a political rival condemns your party, you strike back harder.

It feels natural. But nature is deceptive here. To remain always inside **Your Position** is to remain inside a prison. Pride builds the walls. Anger furnishes the cell.

Opposite Position is the act of breaking out. It is the daring move of **stepping into the shoes of the other side**.

This is not surrender. It is not self-erasure. It is **an act of wisdom**:

- To understand what your spouse, client, or rival sees.
- To discover truths invisible from your own position.
- To release the anger that poisons only yourself.

The paradox is this: when you stop fighting the opposite, and instead become it for a moment, you don't lose yourself. You find a **larger self** — one that sees both sides of the horizon.

2. The Psychology of Opposition

2.1. The Science of Empathy

Inside the brain are **mirror neurons**. When you see someone smile, your brain lights up as if you smiled yourself. When you see someone in pain, your nervous system feels echoes of that pain.

This is the root of empathy: the ability to simulate the experience of others.

By consciously stepping into the Opposite Position, you activate this natural mechanism. You let your brain *mirror* what the other person feels, rather than walling yourself inside pride. The result is not weakness, but clarity.

2.2. Anger as Poison

Anger feels powerful, but it enslaves us. The old Buddhist teaching captures it: *"Holding on to anger is like grasping a hot coal with the intent of throwing it at someone else; you are the one who gets burned."*

To step into the other's position is to drop the coal. The fire cools. Your hands are free again.

2.3. Cognitive Reframing

Psychologists call this **cognitive reframing**: deliberately choosing a new lens.

- *"She insulted me"* becomes *"She was afraid of losing face."*
- *"He betrayed me"* becomes *"He was overwhelmed and made a poor choice."*

Reframing doesn't excuse behavior. It explains it. And explanation is the first step to solution.

3. Family: The Power of Reversal

3.1. The Parent and the Teenager

A father demands:
"If you don't study harder, you'll ruin your future."

The son yells back:
"If you control me like this, I'll never be free!"

Both are trapped in their own position. Each feels unseen.

A therapist intervenes: *"Switch roles."*

The father must now argue as the son:
"I need independence. If you push too hard, I lose myself."

The son must argue as the father:
"I fear your future will collapse if you waste this chance."

Something shifts. Tears come. Neither has surrendered. But each has felt the other's fear. The room softens. A bridge appears.

3.2. Marriage Quarrels

A wife shouts: *"You don't care about me!"*
The husband fires back: *"I work every day for this family!"*

Locked in Your Positions, they wound each other.

In therapy, they swap roles. He must speak her words. She must speak his. At first it feels absurd. Then it feels revealing. They begin to cry not for themselves, but for each other.

3.3. Family Exercise: Argue the Opposite
- Choose one recurring argument.
- Each partner must argue the other's position for five minutes.
- The goal is not to win, but to *feel*.
- End with this sentence: *"What surprised me about your view is..."*

This simple reversal cracks walls of pride and lets light in.

4. Business: Opposition as Innovation

4.1. Amazon: Becoming the Customer

Jeff Bezos forced Amazon leaders to step out of their egos. He said: *"Start with the customer and work backward."*

Instead of Your Position (what Amazon wanted) or Opposite Position (what competitors did), Bezos insisted executives live inside the customer's frustrations.

- Customers hated waiting → Prime.
- Customers wanted everything → Marketplace.
- Customers needed digital infrastructure → AWS.

Opposition — the customer's eyes — built a trillion-dollar empire.

4.2. Apple: Jobs as Consumer

Steve Jobs did not ask engineers what was possible. He asked: *"What would delight the customer?"* He lived inside the opposite's irritation:

- Carrying CDs was annoying → iPod.
- Tiny keyboards were clunky → iPhone.

Opposition is not surrender. It is visionary empathy.

4.3. Tesla: Thinking Like an Environmentalist

Elon Musk did not start with cars. He started with the fears of environmentalists, the frustration of climate scientists, the dream of a cleaner world. Tesla succeeded because it imagined the future through the eyes of its critics of oil.

4.4. Toyota: Kaizen as Opposition

At Toyota, every worker could stop the line with the **Andon cord**. This institutionalized opposition. The system itself demanded that managers hear what workers saw. Opposite voices were not threats — they were the fuel of improvement.

4.5. Business Exercise: Opposition Audit

- Write your top three customer complaints.
- Pretend to be that customer. Write their speech.
- Ask: *What opportunity is hidden inside this complaint?*

Opposition is not your enemy. It is your most honest consultant.

5. Politics: Opposition as the Path to Peace

5.1. Chile: Saying "No" with Joy

In 1988, Chile faced a referendum: yes or no to extend dictatorship. The regime expected fear. The opposition did the unexpected. They campaigned with joy. Music, laughter, humor. They stepped into the dictator's opposite: instead of anger, they offered hope.

People voted "No." Democracy returned without civil war.

5.2. Poland: Roundtable Talks

The Solidarity movement clashed with the communist state. Each side prepared for war. Then they met at a roundtable. Mediators forced them to articulate the other's fear. Workers realized the government feared collapse. The government realized workers feared endless oppression. By voicing each other's terror, they built common ground.

5.3. Mandela: Speaking as the Jailers

Nelson Mandela, after 27 years in prison, could have chosen revenge. Instead, he stepped into the shoes of his jailers. He told them: *"You are afraid of losing everything. But in the new South Africa, you will have a place."*

This empathy was not weakness. It prevented civil war.

5.4. Taiwan: Integrating the Opposition

In Taiwan's transition, the ruling party legalized opposition parties and allowed them into institutions. Instead of silencing rivals, they gave them seats at the table. Democracy survived because opposition was integrated, not crushed.

5.5. When Opposition is Killed

Authoritarian regimes silence rivals, censor press, jail critics. At first, stability looks strong. But beneath, resentment grows. Without opposition, society has no mirror. When eruption comes, it is violent.

6. Wisdom Traditions

6.1. Buddhism: Anger Burns the Holder

Buddhist psychology teaches: anger harms the one who holds it. To step into the opposite is to cool the fire. But caution: compassion does not mean erasing justice.

6.2. Stoicism: The View from Above

Stoics practiced imagining themselves from above, seeing life as if from the stars. From that height, no ego matters. Opposition is simply another part of the whole.

6.3. Zhuangzi: Equalizing Things

The Daoist Zhuangzi laughed at rigid categories. He wrote of a butterfly who dreamed he was a man. Was he a man dreaming of a butterfly, or a butterfly dreaming of a man? The lesson: perspective is fluid. Opposition is a mirror, not an enemy.

7. Surfing Opposition Without Losing Rights

Opposite Position must not be confused with surrender. To forgive does not mean to accept abuse. To empathize does not mean to erase dignity.

The key is balance:
- Anchor your rights.
- Extend empathy.
- Negotiate with calm, not rage.

Mandela forgave, but he built a constitution. Families forgive, but set boundaries. Businesses empathize with customers, but maintain sustainability.

8. Exercises

1. **Role-Play Switch**
In your next conflict, argue as the other person.
2. **Devil's Advocate Journal**
Once a week, write one page defending a view you dislike.
3. **Forgive First, Negotiate Second**
Before demanding change, calm your anger.

9. Closing

Opposite Position is the hardest to enter, but the most liberating.

- Families grow deeper trust.
- Businesses discover innovation.
- Societies achieve peace without blood.

The door to harmony is not in defeating the opposite, but in **becoming it briefly** — with courage, with dignity, with wisdom.

☞ Opposition is not your enemy. It is your teacher.

Chapter 4

Surfing the Three Positions: From Conflict to Strategy

1. Why Surfing Matters

(rephrased opening for stronger impact)

Conflict is not a storm to avoid — it is a wave to ride. A wave will knock down those who stiffen, but it will carry those who know how to move. Surfing the three positions is this art of movement.

Every conflict begins in Your Position. Emotions flare, identity is defended, pride is at stake. If you stay here, anger consumes you. If you step sideways into Neutral Position, you find the anchor of facts — but if you stay here too long, you risk paralysis, stuck in analysis. Only by daring to ride into Opposite Position — the eyes of the other — can you finally reach the shore of common ground.

2. Family Surfing

2.1. The Curfew Battle (Expanded Dialogue)

It was 10:30 when Anna walked in. Her father, Mr. Chen, had been pacing for half an hour.

Father (Your Position, angry):
"Do you think this house is a hotel? I told you ten o'clock sharp! You just don't care about me or your mother!"

Anna (Your Position, defensive):
"I'm seventeen! My friends all stay out later. You treat me like I'm twelve. You don't trust me at all!"

The air tightened. Each clung to their own world. Both "right," both unheard.

Mrs. Chen, calmer, suggested a pause.
"Let's try to do it differently. Let's surf."

Father (shifting to Neutral Position):

"Fact: You agreed to come back at 10. It's now 10:30."

Anna (Neutral Position, nodding reluctantly):
"Yes. Fact: I am 30 minutes late."

The tension softened slightly. Now Mrs. Chen guided them to the third step.

Father (Opposite Position, trying):
"If I were seventeen... I would want freedom. I'd want to prove I can handle myself."

Anna (Opposite Position, slowly):
"If I were Dad... I would be worried something happened. I'd imagine an accident on the bus, or worse."

The room fell quiet. Suddenly, both saw the invisible fear behind the shouting.

Anna (renewed Your Position, calmer):
"I do want more freedom. But I can text if I'll be late."

Father (renewed Your Position, softened):
"I do want you safe. Let's agree on a call. Freedom for you, peace for me."

The conflict ended not in victory, but in balance.

2.2. Marriage Conflict (Expanded)

David and Maria had been married for ten years. Money was always their battleground.

Maria (Your Position, frustrated):
"You never talk to me before buying things. Another gadget? Another waste!"

David (Your Position, defensive):
"I work hard. I deserve something for myself. You act like a dictator over every dollar."

They had repeated this cycle for years.

In therapy, their counselor forced a surf.

Maria (Neutral Position):

"Fact: You bought a $500 drone yesterday. Fact: We did not discuss it."

David (Neutral Position):
"Fact: I used my bonus money. Fact: Our savings goal was $2,000, and now we are $500 short."

The argument shifted — from accusation to fact.

Now, role switch.

Maria (Opposite Position, as David):
"I work long hours. Buying something fun feels like breathing after stress. I need small freedoms."

David (Opposite Position, as Maria):
"I manage the bills. Every surprise expense feels like a betrayal of our plan. I want security."

Maria began crying. "I didn't know you felt suffocated."
David whispered: "I didn't realize you felt so unsafe."

That day, they created a new rule: a "$200 free zone" — each could spend under that without asking. Over $200 required a talk.

Surfing gave them a marriage surfboard.

2.3. Workplace Conflict

At BrightTech, a small startup, tensions grew between engineers and sales.

Sales Manager (Your Position):
"You engineers keep delaying features! I can't close deals!"

Engineer (Your Position):
"You promise impossible deadlines just to get commissions. Then we look incompetent."

The CEO intervened. "Surf it."
- Neutral Position (facts):
- Sales: "Three clients left because we didn't deliver promised features."
- Engineering: "Two features failed because requirements were unclear."

- Opposite Position:
- Sales (as engineers): "We feel pressured to meet promises we didn't agree to."
- Engineers (as sales): "We feel humiliated losing deals because we look too slow."

Common ground emerged: a new rule that sales could not promise features until engineering signed off. Both sides relaxed.

3. Business Surfing Expanded

(additions building on Amazon, Netflix, Toyota already covered in Ch. 2 & 3)

Case: Southwest Airlines
Instead of maximizing profit per seat, they surfed into the opposite's mind: the everyday traveler. Customers wanted reliability, humor, simplicity. By becoming the opposite of stiff, formal airlines, Southwest created loyalty and profitability.

Case: Pixar
Pixar's "Braintrust" meetings force directors to face the opposite. A new film is screened, and peers criticize bluntly. The director must sit in the opposite chair: hearing flaws without defensiveness. This surfing has produced some of the most creative films in history.

4. Political & Social Surfing Expanded

4.1. Chile (Detailed)

General Pinochet expected fear. The opposition instead surfed into the people's exhaustion.
- Your Position: Dictatorship says: "Order or chaos."
- Neutral: Fact: referendum allowed.
- Opposite: People want joy, not endless fear.

The "No" campaign released cheerful ads: children laughing, music, the slogan "Chile, la alegría ya viene" ("Chile, joy is coming"). Instead of anger, they offered hope. They surfed emotions to common ground. The dictatorship lost without war.

4.2. Taiwan (Detailed)

Taiwan's democratization (1980s–1990s) could have exploded. The ruling party (KMT) feared losing power; opposition wanted freedom.

Surfing occurred through:
- Neutral institutions: election commissions, courts.
- Opposite Position: ruling elites understood that allowing opposition inside was safer than silencing them.
- Common Ground: gradual reform. Opposition gained legitimacy, the ruling party kept dignity, and Taiwan transitioned peacefully into democracy.

4.3. Poland (Detailed)

The Polish Roundtable Talks (1989) remain a masterclass in surfing.
- Workers: "We demand rights."
- Government: "We fear collapse and Soviet retaliation."
- Neutral: "The economy is failing; strikes cannot continue."

By voicing each other's fears, they built compromise: partly free elections, gradual reforms. Within a year, democracy emerged. Poland surfed the impossible wave — from dictatorship to democracy without civil war.

4.4. Mandela (Detailed)

Mandela spent 27 years in prison. His anger could have burned him alive. Instead, he surfed.
- Your Position: "My people were oppressed. Justice is owed."
- Neutral: "Fact: whites own the economy, control the military."
- Opposite: "They fear extinction if we rise in revenge."

Mandela offered reconciliation: a Truth and Reconciliation Commission, a constitution protecting both sides. He invited his jailers to his inauguration. By surfing, he turned vengeance into peace.

5. Common Ground Revisited

The shore after surfing is common ground. It is not compromise born of weakness. It is synthesis born of wisdom.

- Families → call when late = freedom + safety.
- Couples → $200 free zone = freedom + security.
- Companies → cross-team rule = trust + efficiency.
- Nations → roundtable = dignity + democracy.

6. Expanded Exercises

Family: "Switch Scripts" night — argue your partner's or child's role in a conflict until they feel understood.
Workplace: "Opposite Chair" rule — in every meeting, one person must argue the customer's or competitor's perspective.
Politics: "Mirror Debate" — each side must begin by summarizing the other's position fairly before presenting their own.

7. Closing

Surfing is wisdom in motion. It is Mandela stepping into the shoes of his jailers. It is a father speaking as a teenager, a wife speaking as her husband, a CEO speaking as the customer.

Rigid minds drown in waves. Surfers ride them to the shore of peace.

 To surf is not to lose yourself. It is to discover the larger self — one that holds truth, empathy, and dignity together.

Surfing the Three Positions → Common Ground

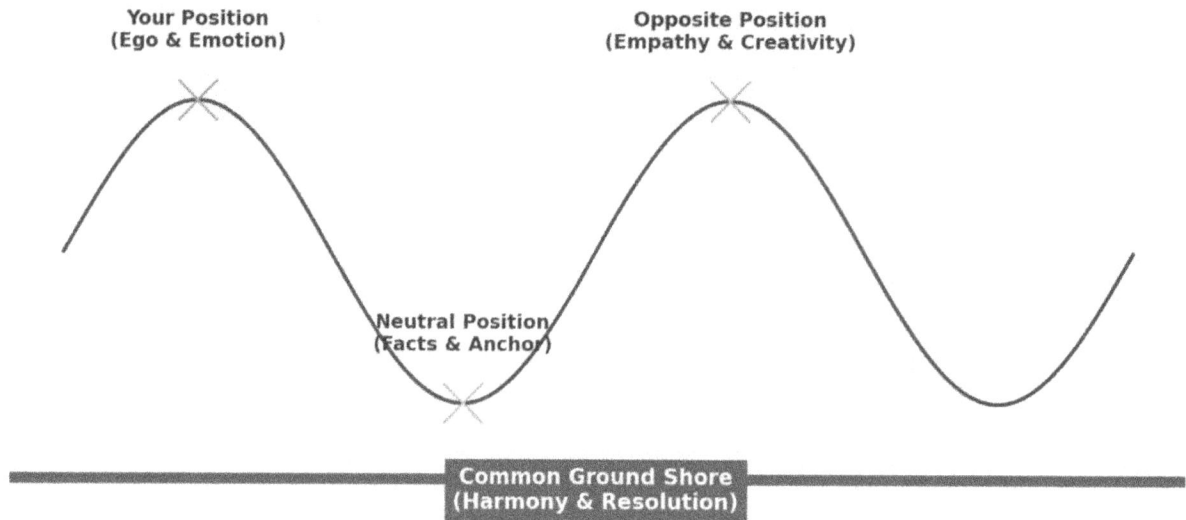

Your Position
(Ego & Emotion)

Opposite Position
(Empathy & Creativity)

Neutral Position
(Facts & Anchor)

Common Ground Shore
(Harmony & Resolution)

Here's the Surfing Wave Diagram for Chapter 4 🌊 **:**

- Your Position (Ego & Emotion) → the starting point on the wave.

- Neutral Position (Facts & Anchor) → dip of balance, stabilizing against ego.

- Opposite Position (Empathy & Creativity) → crest again, opening new vision.

- All movement flows toward the Common Ground Shore (Harmony & Resolution) at the bottom.

👉 This matches the metaphor: you don't stay still — you ride the wave, shifting between positions until you reach harmony.

Surfing the Three Positions → Common Ground

Caption:

Conflict is a wave. If we stiffen, we drown. If we surf, we grow.

- Your Position (Ego & Emotion): the first wave crest, where identity and feelings dominate.

- Neutral Position (Facts & Anchor): the dip of clarity, where truth steadies the mind.

- Opposite Position (Empathy & Creativity): the second crest, where imagination and understanding expand perspective.

- Common Ground Shore: the landing place of wisdom, where conflicts transform into harmony and solutions.

Triangle of Three Positions

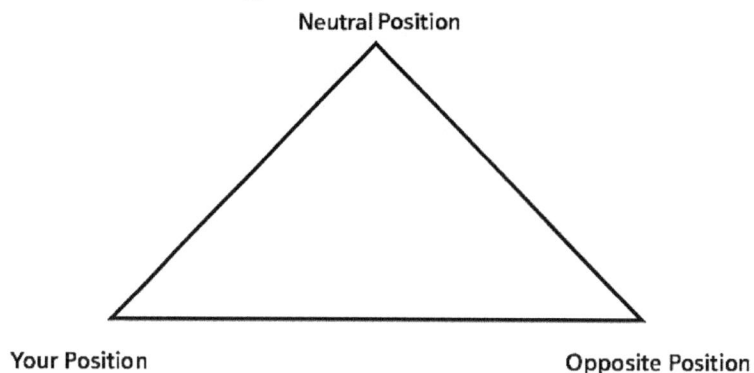

Neutral Position

Your Position   **Opposite Position**

Three distinct perspectives Your Position (ego/self). Neutral Position (facts).
Opposito Position (empathy). True clarity comes from recognizing
all three.

Surfing the Three Positions (Wave)

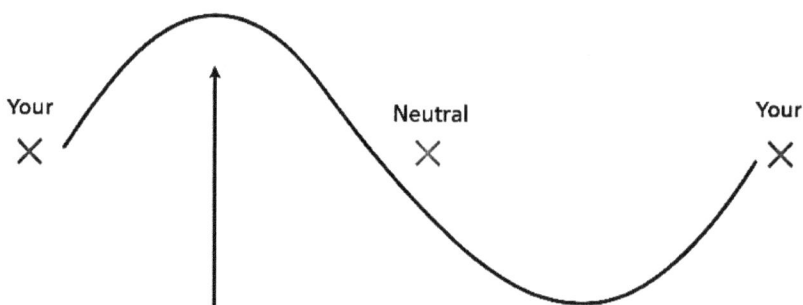

Your   Neutral   Your
X   X   X

Surfing means moving dynamically between positions, balancing like a surfer on
waves. Flexibility prevents rigidity and opens the way to insight, innovation.
and balance.

Common Ground Circle

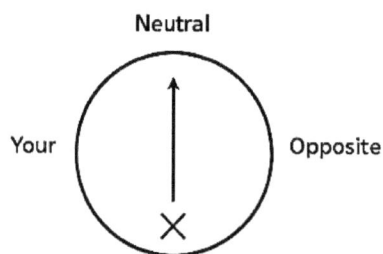

Neutral

Your   Opposite

X

When all three positions are held together, they converge at the center: Common
Ground. This is the seed of peace in families, the foundation of innovation in
business, and the basis of harmony in society.

Surfing Wave Diagram for Chapter 4 🏄 :

- **Your Position (Ego & Emotion)** → the starting point on the wave.
- **Neutral Position (Facts & Anchor)** → dip of balance, stabilizing against ego.
- **Opposite Position (Empathy & Creativity)** → crest again, opening new vision.
- All movement flows toward the **Common Ground Shore (Harmony & Resolution)** at the bottom.

👉 This matches the metaphor: you don't stay still — you ride the wave, shifting between positions until you reach harmony.

Surfing the Three Positions → Common Ground

Caption:

Conflict is a wave. If we stiffen, we drown. If we surf, we grow.

- **Your Position (Ego & Emotion):** the first wave crest, where identity and feelings dominate.
- **Neutral Position (Facts & Anchor):** the dip of clarity, where truth steadies the mind.
- **Opposite Position (Empathy & Creativity):** the second crest, where imagination and understanding expand perspective.
- **Common Ground Shore:** the landing place of wisdom, where conflicts transform into harmony and solutions.

Surfing is not about abandoning the self — it is about riding through all three perspectives with balance until we arrive at peace.

Chapter 5

The Three Positions as a Decision Framework

1. Introduction: From Conflict to Decision

Every decision begins with tension. Should I take the new job? Should the company launch a new product? Should a nation sign a treaty?

Tension exists because there are competing voices: my desire, the facts, and the other side's needs.

Most decisions fail because they get trapped in **one voice only**:

- **Your Position** → Ego-driven decisions (*"I want this, so it must be right"*).
- **Neutral Position** → Paralysis by analysis (*"We have data, but no action"*).
- **Opposite Position** → Over-sympathy (*"We give in to others and neglect ourselves"*).

The **Three Positions Decision Framework** provides a systematic way to move through all three before finalizing choices. The key is not to eliminate conflict, but to **surf it into clarity**.

2. Business Decision-Making

2.1. Amazon AWS: Seeing the Hidden Market

In the early 2000s, Amazon was a retailer drowning in server costs. Internal debates raged: should they build better infrastructure or keep patching?

- **Your Position (internal ego):**
"We are a retailer. Our business is selling books and goods."
- **Neutral Position (facts):**
"Running servers is our biggest bottleneck. We keep reinventing the wheel."
- **Opposite Position (external need):**

"Other companies also suffer the same pain. They would pay for scalable infrastructure."

By considering the **opposite — the client's pain** — Amazon made a radical decision: offer cloud computing to others. The result was **Amazon Web Services (AWS)**, now the most profitable arm of the company.

👉 **Lesson:** Without surfing into the opposite, Amazon would have stayed "just a store."

2.2. Toyota Hybrid Strategy

In the 1990s, Toyota faced a dilemma. Gas cars dominated, but environmental concerns were growing.

- **Your Position (ego):**
"We build reliable gasoline cars. That's who we are."
- **Neutral Position (facts):**
"Fossil fuel dependence is rising. Oil prices are volatile. Regulations are tightening."
- **Opposite Position (critics):**
"Environmentalists and consumers want cleaner cars."

Surfing these three led Toyota to launch the **Prius**, the world's first mass-market hybrid. At first mocked, it became iconic, setting Toyota years ahead in green innovation.

2.3. Netflix Original Content

Netflix began as a DVD rental company. Then they shifted to streaming. But competitors started reclaiming content.

- **Your Position:**
"We are a streaming platform."
- **Neutral:**
"Fact: Licensing costs are rising, dependence on studios is dangerous."
- **Opposite (studios' view):**
"They see us as a threat. They will take content back."

The answer was bold: create original content. *House of Cards, Orange is the New Black, Stranger Things* — all born from surfing the three positions.

2.4. Business Exercise: Decision Surfing Matrix

Create a 3-column table before any big decision:

Your Position	Neutral Position	Opposite Position
What do I/our team want?	What do the facts say?	What does the other side (customer/competitor/partner) want?

Then: ask, *What common ground solution emerges when all three are considered?*

3. Political Decision-Making

3.1. Taiwan's Balancing Act

Taiwan lives in a geopolitical storm. Decisions about independence, trade, and defense are existential.

- **Your Position:**
"We are a sovereign democracy."
- **Neutral:**
"Fact: China is militarily stronger, the U.S. is a security guarantor, our economy depends on both."
- **Opposite (Beijing's fears):**
"They fear losing face and legitimacy if Taiwan declares independence."

By surfing, Taiwan has chosen pragmatic ambiguity: strengthen democracy, deepen global alliances, but avoid direct provocation. This surfing keeps peace while building resilience.

3.2. U.S. Civil Rights Movement

Dr. Martin Luther King Jr. embodied the framework.
- **Your Position:**

"Black Americans deserve equal rights now."
- **Neutral:**

"Fact: The Constitution promises equality. The world is watching America's hypocrisy."
- **Opposite (white fears):**

"They fear violence, loss of control, humiliation."

King's genius was speaking from all three. His *"I Have a Dream"* speech invoked passion (Your), law (Neutral), and reassurance (Opposite). This surfing helped pass the Civil Rights Act.

3.3. Poland's Roundtable: Structured Surfing

At the 1989 Roundtable, decisions were mapped like a matrix:

- Your Position (workers: freedom).
- Neutral (economy collapsing).
- Opposite (government fears chaos and Soviet invasion).

By recognizing all three, they reached historic agreements. Poland became the first Eastern Bloc country to democratize peacefully.

3.4. Political Exercise: Opposition Decision Drill

Choose one hot issue (immigration, healthcare, climate). Write 3 versions of the policy:

- One from Your Position.
- One purely from Neutral facts.
- One from the strongest Opposite view.

Then combine elements into a synthesis.

4. Personal Life Decisions

4.1. Career Choice

- **Your Position:** "I love art. I want to be a designer."
- **Neutral:** "Fact: Designers face tough job markets. Income is unstable."
- **Opposite:** "Employers and clients need practical design that sells."

Surfing these three might produce: become a **UX designer** — creative passion (Your), market demand (Neutral), client needs (Opposite).

4.2. Marriage & Parenting

Scenario: A couple deciding whether to move for a new job.
- **Your Position (wife):** "I want stability for the kids."
- **Your Position (husband):** "I want career growth."
- **Neutral:** "The new job doubles income but requires relocation."
- **Opposite:** "Kids' perspective: fear of losing friends."

Surfing through all four leads to compromise: relocate, but choose a family-friendly area and involve children in decisions.

4.3. Health Decisions

Doctor and patient often clash:

- **Patient's Position:** "I want to avoid surgery."
- **Neutral:** "MRI shows damage."
- **Doctor's Position (Opposite):** "If untreated, it worsens."

Surfing together creates middle ground: minimally invasive procedures, physical therapy first.

4. The 3-Step Decision Method

1. **Write Your Position.**
   - Desires, fears, instincts.

2.   **Extract Neutral Position.**
    - Facts, data, evidence.
3.   **Adopt Opposite Position.**
    - Other's needs, fears, demands.

Then: craft a **Common Ground Decision** that integrates all three.

6. Advanced Applications of the Three Positions Framework

6.1 Negotiations: Surfing Between Unions and Management

Negotiations are often framed as war: management vs. workers, buyers vs. sellers, nations vs. nations. Each side comes in with their **Your Position**: demands, anger, non-negotiables.

But successful negotiations come when both sides **surf across the three positions**.

Example: Auto Industry Union Talks

- **Union's Position:** "We need higher wages, shorter hours, and job security. We cannot survive otherwise."

- **Management's Position:** "We need to reduce costs, increase productivity, and stay competitive."

For decades, these two positions clashed head-on, resulting in strikes, slowdowns, or layoffs.

When they began to **surf**, something changed:

- **Neutral Position (facts):** Data showed global competition rising, automation increasing, and companies like Toyota outperforming because of efficiency.

- **Opposite Position:** Management stepped into workers' shoes — *"If I were on the line, I'd fear losing my home if wages stay flat."* Workers stepped into management's shoes — *"If I were the CEO, I'd fear bankruptcy if costs explode."*

43

Surfing revealed common ground: better wages *tied to productivity gains*. This birthed **profit-sharing models** and **joint efficiency committees**. Workers earned more when the company did well. Companies became leaner without mass layoffs.

👉 **Lesson:** Surfing doesn't erase conflict. It re-channels it into **cooperative creativity**.

6.2 Diplomacy: The Camp David Accords

In 1978, U.S. President Jimmy Carter brought Egyptian President Anwar Sadat and Israeli Prime Minister Menachem Begin to Camp David for peace talks. The Middle East had suffered decades of war.

Both leaders arrived entrenched in **Your Position**:

- **Israel (Your Position):** "We need security and recognition. We cannot withdraw from Sinai unless Egypt guarantees peace."
- **Egypt (Your Position):** "We need sovereignty over our land. Sinai must be returned. Israel must stop settlements."

Talks nearly collapsed. Ego and pride dominated.

Carter forced them to **surf**:

- **Neutral Position (facts):** Maps were drawn. History reviewed. Military realities analyzed. Both sides acknowledged reality: Israel could not be secure without peace, Egypt could not regain dignity without land.

- **Opposite Position:** Sadat was asked, *"If you were Israeli, what would you fear most?"* Begin was asked, *"If you were Egyptian, how would occupation feel?"*

This shift cracked open possibilities.

The **Common Ground Agreement**:

- Israel withdrew from Sinai (Egypt's sovereignty recognized).
- Egypt formally recognized Israel (Israel's security affirmed).

Sadat and Begin both won. Sadat said: *"No more war."* Begin said: *"Peace with the strongest Arab nation."*

👉 **Lesson:** Surfing allowed both sides to leave with dignity, not defeat.

6.3 Crisis Leadership: COVID-19 Responses

The pandemic tested governments worldwide. Each faced an impossible wave: disease, economic collapse, public fear.

Those that failed were stuck in one position:

- **Your Position only (ego/politics):** Leaders downplayed the virus (*"It's just flu"*), prioritizing image. Result: uncontrolled outbreaks.
- **Neutral Position only (facts):** Some leaders listened to scientists but ignored people's emotions. Result: protests, vaccine resistance.
- **Opposite Position only (fear of economy):** Some leaders reopened too fast. Result: new waves of infection.

Those that **surfaced best** balanced all three:

- **Your Position (citizens' fear):** Leaders acknowledged pain and gave reassurance (*"We are in this together"*).
- **Neutral Position (scientific data):** Clear dashboards, evidence-based rules, vaccine logistics.
- **Opposite Position (economic costs):** Support for businesses, relief packages, job subsidies.

Examples:
- **New Zealand:** Surfed effectively. PM Jacinda Ardern spoke empathetically (Your), used science-driven lockdowns (Neutral), and offered economic relief (Opposite). Result: early containment, public trust.

- **Germany:** Surfed at first with fact-based policy + subsidies. Later faltered when stuck in Neutral-only (data-heavy but emotionally cold), showing the need for empathy too.

- **Brazil & U.S. (early pandemic):** Leaders stuck in ego (Your Position denial). Result: high death tolls, mistrust, deeper division.

Lesson: In crisis, surfing is survival. Ego alone kills, facts alone paralyze, empathy alone destabilizes. Only all three together steer nations through storms.

Reflection Questions

1. **Negotiations:** If you're in a union-management conflict, what *opposite fear* is the other side hiding that could open a path to compromise?

2. **Diplomacy:** When nations clash, what *map of neutral facts* would both sides acknowledge if egos were stripped away?

3. **Crisis Leadership:** In today's challenges (climate, pandemics, inequality), how can leaders surf between citizens' fears, hard data, and economic costs without drowning in any single wave?

Closing of Section 6

The Three Positions are not abstract philosophy — they are the **hidden mechanics of history's biggest decisions**.

- Negotiations survive when both sides surf.
- Peace treaties succeed when leaders step into the opposite.
- Crises are managed when fear, facts, and empathy are balanced.

The future will belong to those who can ride these waves.

Union
Wages & Security

Management
Costs & Productivity

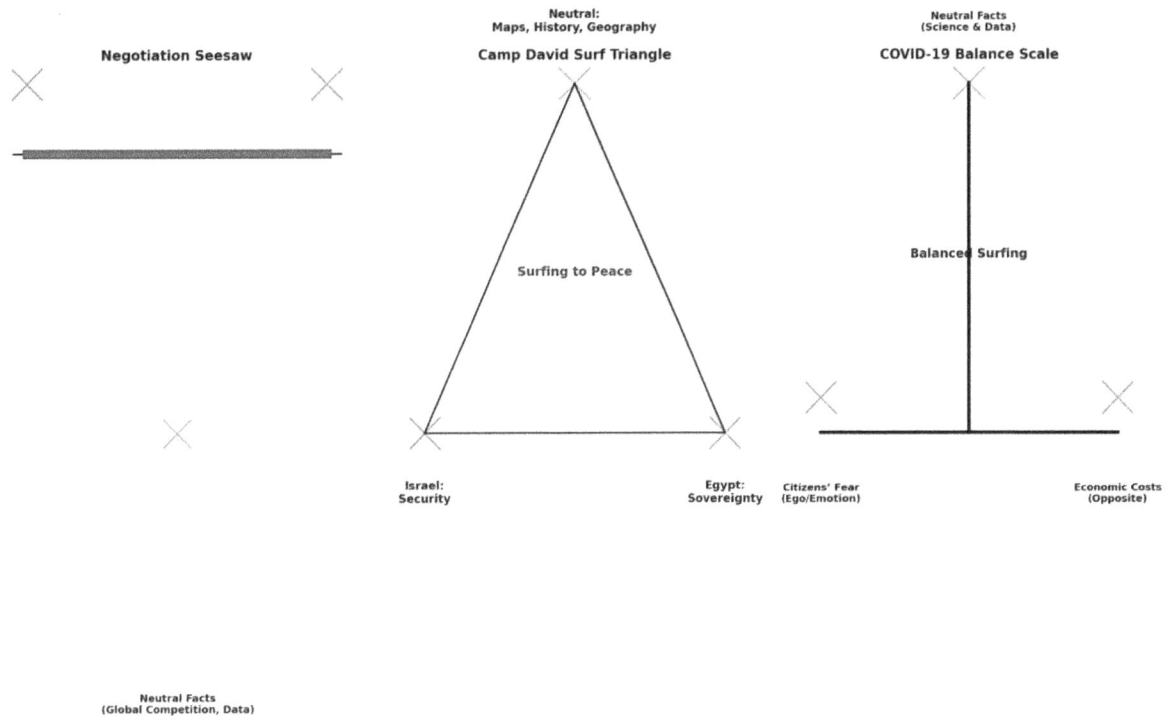

Neutral:
Maps, History, Geography

Neutral Facts
(Science & Data)

Negotiation Seesaw

Camp David Surf Triangle

COVID-19 Balance Scale

Surfing to Peace

Balanced Surfing

Israel:
Security

Egypt:
Sovereignty

Citizens' Fear
(Ego/Emotion)

Economic Costs
(Opposite)

Neutral Facts
(Global Competition, Data)

three diagrams for Section 6 (Advanced Applications):

1. **Negotiation Seesaw**
   - Union on one end, Management on the other.
   - Neutral Facts as the balancing pivot in the middle (global competition, data).

3. **Camp David Surf Triangle** ▲

   - Israel's Security, Egypt's Sovereignty, and Neutral (maps/history/geography) forming a triangle.
   - "Surfing to Peace" in the center.

3. **COVID-19 Balance Scale**

- Citizens' Fear (Your Position), Economic Costs (Opposite), Science & Data (Neutral at the top).
- Balance comes from surfing between them.

Diagram 1 – Negotiation Seesaw

Caption:

Unions and management often sit at opposite ends of a seesaw — one demanding wages, the other fearing costs. The Neutral Position, grounded in facts like global competition and productivity data, becomes the balance point. Surfing across all three transforms stalemate into win-win agreements.

Diagram 2 – Camp David Surf Triangle

Caption:

Israel's security, Egypt's sovereignty, and the Neutral facts of maps and history formed the three corners of the Camp David triangle. Only by surfing between these positions could leaders reach peace — returning land, granting recognition, and preserving dignity for both nations.

Diagram 3 – COVID-19 Balance Scale

Caption:

Crisis leadership means balancing citizens' fear, scientific data, and economic costs. Leaders who surfed among these three positions earned trust and saved lives. Those stuck in only one wave — ego, data alone, or economics — faltered.

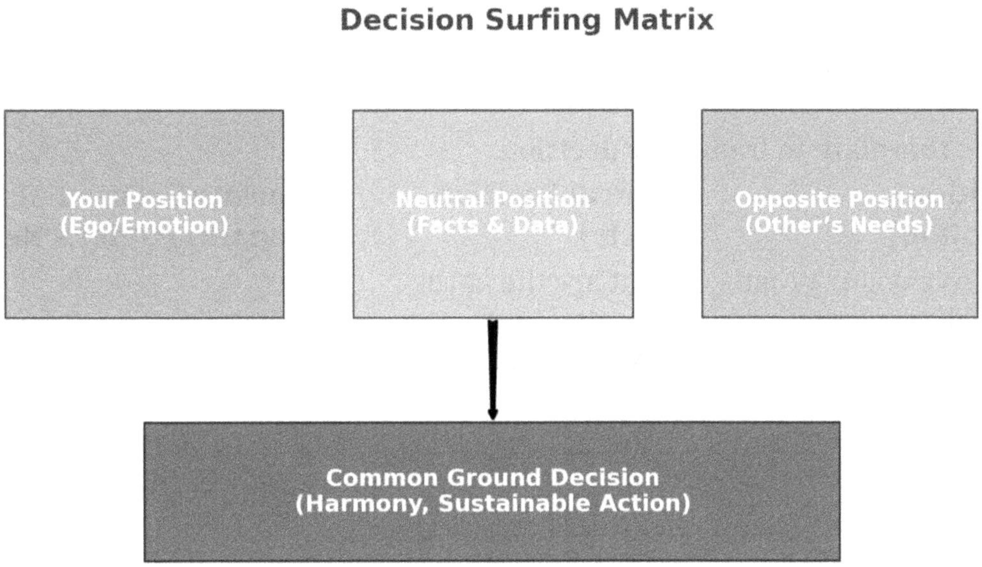

Decision Surfing Matrix Diagram 📝:

- **Three columns** for Your Position, Neutral Position, and Opposite Position.
- Each feeds into an arrow pointing down to the **Common Ground Decision** box.
- Designed to be printable as a **decision template** for meetings, journaling, or family discussions.

Decision-Making Toolkits: From Theory to Daily Practice

Toolkit 1: The Decision Surfing Matrix

A **one-page template** to frame any decision.

Your Position (Ego/Emotion)	Neutral Position (Facts)	Opposite Position (Empathy/Other's Needs)
What do I/we want? What are our desires, fears, instincts?	What are the hard data, timelines, numbers, and facts?	

How to use:

1. Fill each column honestly before deciding.
2. Highlight contradictions.
3. Ask: *What common ground integrates all three?*

- Example: A company debating remote work.
- Your Position: "We want employees in office for culture."
- Neutral: "Productivity data shows remote is stable."
- Opposite: "Employees value flexibility."
- Common Ground: Hybrid model with office anchor days.

Toolkit 2: The Decision Surfing Checklist

Before any major choice, walk through this **7-question checklist**:

1. Have I written down **my own desires and fears** clearly?
2. Have I gathered **neutral facts** (data, timelines, costs, evidence)?
3. Have I considered the **opposite perspective** honestly?
4. What **hidden fears** might the other side carry?
5. What **blind spots** might I have if I only stay in my position?
6. What decision would create **dignity for all sides**?
7. If I decide now, will this lead to **peace and sustainability** — or more conflict later?

- Print this checklist for boardrooms, classrooms, and even kitchen fridges.

Toolkit 3: The Surfing Journal Method

Daily journaling to train the Three Positions as a habit.

- **Step 1: Recall a conflict or decision from the day.**
- **Step 2: Write three paragraphs:**
- One in **Your Position** ("I was angry because…").
- One in **Neutral Position** ("The fact was…").
- One in **Opposite Position** ("If I were them…").
- **Step 3:** Summarize the **common ground** insight you discovered.

👉 Example:
- Your Position: "My colleague ignored my email. Disrespectful!"
- Neutral: "Fact: It was Monday morning, 200 unread emails."
- Opposite: "If I were them, I'd feel overwhelmed."
- Common Ground: "I'll call next time instead of emailing."

Over weeks, this rewires perception: you naturally surf in real time.

Toolkit 4: The Decision Surfboard Map (Visual)

A **visual canvas** for teams:

- Left Wave Crest = Your Position (desires, ego).
- Valley = Neutral Position (facts, reality check).
- Right Crest = Opposite Position (other's needs).
- Shore = Common Ground (decision).

Teams can sketch this on whiteboards during meetings.

👉 Example: Product launch decision. The wave map shows each side, then the landing.

Toolkit 5: Opposite Chair Role-Play

Especially powerful for teams or families.
- Assign someone to argue the **Opposite Position** of the main decision.
- Another to hold **Neutral Position** (fact-checker).

- Another to stay in **Your Position**.
- Rotate roles until all three have been voiced.

This forces empathy and reveals hidden insights.

☞ Example: A union negotiation role-play where managers must argue as workers, and vice versa, often cracks deadlocks.

Toolkit 6: Fact-Check Drill

Training to separate ego from evidence.

- Write your desired decision.
- Underline every statement that is **fact**.
- Circle every statement that is **opinion or fear**.
- Revise until facts and fears are clearly separated.

☞ Example: "We must expand to Asia this year."

- Fact: Competitor revenue is growing in Asia.
- Opinion: "We'll fail if we don't."
- Fear: "Our board will think we are weak."

The drill helps leaders see **what's real** vs. **what's emotional noise**.

Toolkit 7: Decision Debrief Ritual

After any big decision, conduct a short debrief:

- Did we honor Your, Neutral, and Opposite?
- Which position dominated too much?
- Did we truly land on Common Ground?

This builds organizational learning and prevents ego capture.

Toolkit 8: Surfing for Families & Couples

A home version:

- Keep a **"Three Position Board"** on the fridge.
- Each family member writes:
- "My position is…"
- "The fact is…"
- "If I were you, I'd feel…"
- Once a week, review and resolve.

👉 Parents report kids become more empathetic — arguments cool faster because everyone feels heard.

Closing of Toolkit Section

Frameworks matter only if they are **usable daily**. The checklists, journals, and role-plays here make surfing not just theory but practice.

The real power of the Three Positions is not in occasional breakthroughs, but in **habitual use**. Like a surfer who trains balance every day, wise decision-makers strengthen by practicing, reflecting, and repeating.

Chapter 6

Surfing the Self: Personal Growth and Leadership Transformation

1. Introduction: Why Leaders Fail Without Surfing

Leadership is not simply about making decisions. It is about **holding tensions without breaking**. Parents, managers, presidents, even community volunteers — all face the same waves: ego, facts, and empathy.

When leaders fail, it is usually because they get **stuck** in one position:

- **Your Position (ego/authority only):** The authoritarian father, the tyrant CEO, the dictator. They demand loyalty but generate fear and resentment.
- **Neutral Position (facts only):** The technocrat who knows statistics but cannot inspire people. They design perfect spreadsheets but lose the hearts of those they lead.
- **Opposite Position (empathy only):** The over-sympathetic leader who bends so much they disappear. They sacrifice their own people's dignity, or their own self-respect.

History is filled with such failures. But leaders who learn to **surf all three positions** — shifting between self, facts, and empathy — discover a rare kind of strength: **wisdom in action**.

2. Personal Growth: Training the Inner Surfer

Surfing the Three Positions begins not in boardrooms or parliaments, but in **self-awareness**.

2.1. Recognizing Triggers

Each of us has a "default trap."

- Some cling to **ego** — "I must win every argument."
- Some hide in **facts** — "I'll bury myself in research so I don't have to feel."
- Some overextend empathy — "I'll keep forgiving, even if I'm destroyed."

The first step is to **name your trap**.

👉 Reflection Question: *When conflict arises, do I defend myself, retreat into data, or collapse into pleasing others?*

2.2. Building Humility for Neutral Position

Neutrality requires humility. It means admitting: *My view may not be the whole truth.*

Exercises:

- Daily fact-checking journal: write one assumption, and then research if it's true.
- Family practice: in any dispute, stop and state one shared fact before arguing.

2.3. Building Empathy for Opposite Position

Empathy is not weakness. It is strength to imagine the enemy's fears without surrendering your own dignity.
Exercises:

- Role reversal: once a week, argue your spouse's or colleague's viewpoint sincerely.
- Media surf: read an article from a political stance opposite to yours — write one insight you gained.

2.4. Integrating All Three

True surfing = fluidity. It's like breath: inhale (Your), hold (Neutral), exhale (Opposite). You cannot survive with only one.

3. Leadership Transformation

Great leadership is surfing applied in public.

3.1. Abraham Lincoln

- **Your Position:** preserve the Union.
- **Neutral Position:** reality of slavery, constitutional law, battlefield data.
- **Opposite Position:** southern fears of annihilation.

Lincoln's genius was balancing all three — firm on principle, pragmatic on law, empathetic in rhetoric. His Gettysburg Address is pure surfing: honoring the dead, grounding in fact, inviting reconciliation.

3.2. Angela Merkel

Known as "Mutti" (mother) of Germany, Merkel embodied Neutral Position (scientist, data-driven). But she never lost empathy (welcoming refugees in 2015), nor ego (protecting German interests in EU debt crisis). Surfing made her Europe's anchor for 16 years.

3.3. Nelson Mandela Revisited

Mandela's surfing is unparalleled:

- Your Position: "We deserve justice."
- Neutral: "The white minority still holds weapons."
- Opposite: "They fear revenge."

By surfing, Mandela avoided civil war. He taught the world that forgiveness is not surrender, but strategy.

4. Workplace Leadership: Surfing in Teams

Modern workplaces are surfboards.

Case: Tech Startup Conflict

Product team says: "We need more time to test." Sales says: "We need to ship now."

A weak leader picks one side.
A strong leader surfs:
- Your Position: company survival.
- Neutral: market data, revenue runway.
- Opposite: customer frustrations, worker burnout.

Decision: phased launch — a partial release that satisfies sales, while protecting product integrity.

☞ Surfing builds **trust and innovation** because every voice feels heard.

5. Family & Parenting: Surfing as Daily Practice

Surfing is not just for CEOs. It is for dinner tables.

5.1. Parents as Surfers

Authoritarian parent = "Because I said so."
Permissive parent = "Whatever you want."
Surfing parent = "I hear you, here are the facts, here's how we meet halfway."

5.2. Marriage as a Surfboard

In marriage, surfing prevents escalation.
Example: one spouse wants to save money, the other wants vacation.

- Your: "I deserve this trip."
- Neutral: "Bank account = $5,000."
- Opposite: "They crave rest, or they crave security."

Surfing lands on a common ground: maybe a smaller vacation, or save now/travel later plan.

6. Advanced Training: Building Surfing Habits

6.1. Daily Surf Journal

Every evening, replay one conflict with three lenses. Over time, it rewires your instincts.

6.2. Surf Pause Technique

When anger rises, pause. Say silently: *My view, the facts, their view.* Then respond.

6.3. Leadership Surf Drill

In meetings, leaders should explicitly ask:

1. What's our position?
2. What are the facts?
3. What would our customers or rivals say?

6.4. Family Surf Circle

Weekly ritual: each family member shares one fact, one feeling, one empathy perspective. Children raised in surf families become resilient adults.

7. Obstacles to Surfing

1.   **Over-Sympathy:** Always bending → loss of rights. Solution: affirm Your Position firmly before empathy.
2.   **Data Obsession:** Cold reliance on Neutral → soulless decisions. Solution: add human cost analysis.
3.   **Ego Rigidity:** Stuck in Your → endless conflict. Solution: force fact-checking, role reversal.

Surfing is not about balance at every moment. It's about flow across traps.

8. Surfing as Wisdom-in-Action

Surfing is not compromise. It is **dynamic wisdom**.

- Leaders use it to unite nations.
- Parents use it to raise resilient children.
- Couples use it to sustain love.
- Individuals use it to find peace.

Surfing the Three Positions is not merely a technique — it is a way of being.

It means living not as a rigid fortress, but as a flowing surfer: grounded in self, anchored in fact, expanded by empathy, always moving toward harmony.

Chapter 7

Surfing Global Waves: The Three Positions in World Challenges

1. Introduction: Why Global Problems Defy Single Positions

The 21st century presents humanity with challenges larger than any nation or individual can resolve alone. Climate change, pandemics, artificial intelligence, inequality, and war are not "local storms." They are planetary waves.

Yet, our current responses often fail because they are **locked in one position**:

- **Your Position (national ego):** Nations defend short-term self-interest. "Our jobs first. Our energy first. Our security first."
- **Neutral Position (data obsession):** Scientists and economists deliver perfect graphs and warnings, but their truth alone cannot motivate political courage.
- **Opposite Position (empathy only):** Calls to "save the world" by abandoning sovereignty often alienate those who feel unheard.

The result: paralysis. Summits end with photo ops. Agreements lack teeth. Citizens despair at endless talk.

To solve global challenges, we must learn to **surf all three positions together** — individually, nationally, and institutionally. The Three Positions is not only a tool for family or business. It is a **blueprint for civilization**.

2. Climate Change: Surfing Between Fear, Data, and Responsibility

2.1. The Ego Trap: Your Position

For decades, climate negotiations have collapsed because each nation clings to ego:
- **U.S.:** "We won't sacrifice jobs."
- **China & India:** "We must grow; don't limit us like you already grew."
- **Oil states:** "We depend on fossil fuels for survival."

Every nation has reasons, but when all defend ego alone, emissions rise.

2.2. The Neutral Anchor: Science

The Intergovernmental Panel on Climate Change (IPCC) has delivered report after report. Data is clear: temperatures rise, seas rise, disasters intensify. The Neutral Position is undeniable.

But facts alone do not move hearts. Leaders return home to voters who say: "Science doesn't pay my bills."

2.3. The Opposite Lens: Vulnerable Nations

Imagine being the Maldives or Kiribati, island nations facing extinction. Their Opposite Position is raw: *"If you keep polluting, we disappear."*
Or farmers in Africa who did nothing to cause warming but lose crops to drought.

By entering their perspective, the world feels the **human urgency** beyond data.

2.4. Surfing Toward Common Ground

The **Paris Agreement (2015)** was imperfect but historic because it surfed:
- Nations kept **Your Position** sovereignty (voluntary pledges).
- It anchored in **Neutral data** (2°C target).
- It acknowledged **Opposite fears** (finance for developing nations).

Surfing allowed fragile consensus.

Lesson: The path to net-zero requires surfing every step — industry's survival, scientific truth, and vulnerable people's dignity.

3. Technology & AI Ethics: Balancing Innovation and Humanity

3.1. The Ego Trap: Tech Giants

Silicon Valley often speaks from ego: "Move fast, break things, dominate the market." Profit and power dominate Your Position.

3.2. Neutral Anchor: The Data of Risk

Studies show AI systems can entrench bias, enable surveillance, and disrupt jobs. Neutral Position warns us: the risks are measurable. The EU AI Act, UNESCO ethics frameworks, and countless academic reports anchor this truth.

3.3. Opposite Position: Citizens' Fears

Imagine being a teenager whose every click is tracked, or a worker fearing replacement. Citizens' Opposite Position screams: *"We are not test subjects. We are humans."*

3.4. Surfing to Sustainable Tech

The best companies now surf consciously:
- Microsoft and Google fund AI ethics boards (Neutral).
- Governments push regulations to protect citizens (Opposite).
- Tech firms still pursue innovation (Your Position).

When aligned, surfing produces **Responsible AI**: growth with guardrails.

☞ **Lesson:** Innovation must surf — otherwise it becomes tyranny of code.

4. Inequality & Economic Justice

4.1. The Ego Trap: Elites and Governments

The wealthy defend tax shelters; governments defend "fiscal discipline." Your Position often sounds like: *"If we tax too much, investment flees."*

4.2. Neutral Anchor: Data on Inequality

The Neutral facts are stark: the richest 1% own more than half of global wealth. Middle classes shrink. Future generations inherit debt and instability.

4.3. Opposite Position: The Poor and Excluded

The working poor, informal workers, migrants — their Opposite Position says: *"We cannot wait decades. We are drowning now."*

4.4. Surfing Toward Justice

Some nations surf better:

- **Nordic welfare models**: dignity for all, competitive economies.
- **Universal Basic Income pilots**: giving dignity + data-driven evaluation.
- **Latin America's lesson**: empathy alone without Neutral economics often collapsed into inflation.

☞ **Lesson:** Surfing inequality means joining dignity, data, and responsibility.

5. War & Peace: International Surfing

5.1. When Surfing Fails → War

The Russia–Ukraine war is a case of ego dominance. Russia's Your Position ("historic destiny") ignored Neutral facts (economic collapse, NATO resolve) and Opposite fears (Ukraine's right to exist). War is the cost of refusing to surf.

5.2. When Surfing Succeeds → Peace

- **Northern Ireland: Good Friday Agreement (1998).**
- Your Position: Unionists wanted UK identity. Nationalists wanted Irish unity.
- Neutral: decades of bloodshed, stalemate.
- Opposite: families on both sides grieving.
- Surfing birthed shared institutions — peace endures.
- **South Korea's Sunshine Policy (2000s).**
- Your Position: South Korea's security.
- Neutral: economic gaps and North's military risk.
- Opposite: North Korea's fear of collapse.
- Surfing created family reunions, aid, dialogue. Imperfect, but it cooled war.
- **Camp David revisited:** Already discussed in Chapter 5, but here stands as proof that **surfing even bitter enemies can transform decades of blood into coexistence.**

☞ **Lesson:** Peace = surfing past ego into shared humanity.

6. Institutions as Surfboards for the World

6.1. UN, EU, WHO as Neutral Anchors

These institutions are attempts to anchor the world in Neutral Position. They gather facts, moderate debates, provide rules.

But they often lack **Your Position strength** (enforcement) and **Opposite empathy** (representation of the powerless). Result: distrust and gridlock.

6.2. The Need for Stronger Surfboards

We need **surfboards at planetary scale**:
- Institutions that balance ego (national interest), Neutral (science), and Opposite (humanity's weakest).
- Possible vision: a **Global Surf Charter** where every major issue must be debated explicitly through all three positions.

☞ Example: A Climate Surf Council where oil states, scientists, and island nations sit together — each position voiced before policy.

7. Exercises for Global Citizens

The world's future does not rest only on leaders. Citizens can train themselves as surfers too.

1. **Climate Surf Drill:**

   - Your: "I like driving my car."
   - Neutral: "CO_2 emissions accelerate warming."
   - Opposite: "Future generations will inherit disaster."
   - Common ground: switch to hybrid or public transit weekly.

2. **Tech Surf Drill:**

   - Your: "I enjoy free social media."
   - Neutral: "Data shows addiction, privacy loss."
   - Opposite: "My children will suffer mental health decline."

- Common ground: set limits, push for privacy-friendly apps.

4.   **Inequality Surf Drill:**

- Your: "I work hard for my salary."
- Neutral: "The wealth gap is unsustainable."
- Opposite: "Billions live on $2/day."
- Common ground: support fair taxation, donate, advocate.

The point is simple: **global surfing begins at home.**

8. Closing: The Ocean of Humanity

Humanity is riding the greatest wave in history. Never before have we had such power — to warm a planet, build machines that think, concentrate wealth, or annihilate nations.

The choice is simple:

- Ride only **Your Position**, and drown in ego-driven wars and destruction.
- Hide in **Neutral data**, and watch paralysis rot the world.
- Collapse into **Opposite empathy alone**, and lose stability.

Or — surf all three, together.

The Three Positions is not just a philosophy of family peace or workplace leadership. It is a **civilizational survival skill**.

If we can learn to surf — as citizens, as nations, as a species — then the waves of climate, technology, inequality, and war will not drown us. They will carry us toward the **Common Ground Shore of peace, dignity, and sustainability.**

(Expanded: Religious Authoritarianism in Islamic Contexts)

Ego Cultures

Ego cultures emerge wherever authority is absolute, dissent is equated with betrayal, and identity is enforced as loyalty. While Confucian hierarchy and fascist nationalism are classic forms, another enduring type is **religious authoritarian governance** in parts of the Islamic world.

A. **Religious Authoritarianism:**

   Faith as Political Ego

   • **When religion is fused with state power**, faith ceases to be a personal or communal path and becomes an instrument of political control.

   • Leaders or clerics claim to embody divine will; therefore, opposing them equals opposing God.

   • Neutral data (economics, science, human rights law) is dismissed as "Western" or "corrupted."

   • Opposite voices (minorities, women, dissidents, secular citizens) are silenced under charges of heresy or blasphemy.

Examples in practice:

   • **Iran (post-1979):** Supreme Leader claims ultimate authority, making all other institutions subordinate. Ego: clerical rule. Neutral: economic mismanagement hidden. Opposite: women, minorities, protesters suppressed.

   • **Taliban's Afghanistan:** Religious purity overruled Neutral (schooling, economic data) and Opposite (women's rights, ethnic groups). The result: long-term instability.

   • **Saudi Arabia's Wahhabi tradition (20th century):** Religious police enforced rigid moral codes; dissent crushed. Recently, partial reforms introduced Neutral pragmatism, but Ego remains dominant.

Why it fails:

- **Rigidity**: When divine will is monopolized by rulers, no correction is possible without theological rebellion.

- **Blindness**: Neutral evidence is ignored; data on health, economy, climate, and education are censored if inconvenient.

- **Exclusion**: Empathy is restricted to "the faithful," leaving others invisible.

Thus, like nationalism or Confucian hierarchy, religious authoritarianism is an **ego culture**: powerful, cohesive, but brittle and self-destructive.

B. Surfing Potentials Inside Islamic Civilization

It is crucial not to equate Islam itself with authoritarian ego. **Within Islamic history and philosophy, powerful surfing traditions exist** that point toward balance.

1. **Sufism (Mystical Islam).**

   - Focuses on humility, self-emptying, and union with the divine.
   - Surfing resonance: Ego (self-centeredness) is deconstructed, Neutral (facts of impermanence) is embraced, Opposite (love for all beings) is institutionalized in poetry, rituals, and service.
   - Rumi's poetry: *"Out beyond ideas of wrongdoing and rightdoing there is a field. I'll meet you there."* — a surfing vision of common ground.

2. **Andalusian Spain (8th–15th centuries).**

   - In medieval Córdoba and Granada, Muslim, Christian, and Jewish scholars coexisted and co-created.
   - Surfing in practice: Ego (Islamic rule) balanced with Neutral (Greek-Arabic science, philosophy) and Opposite (plural communities).

•   This produced breakthroughs in medicine, astronomy, and philosophy, later fueling the European Renaissance.

3.   **Modern Islamic Surfing Efforts.**
    •   Indonesia: Though imperfect, its democracy integrates Islamic values with pluralist governance.
    •   Tunisia's Arab Spring: The most successful early experiment in balancing religious identity with democratic Neutral anchors and Opposite protections for women.

B. Lessons: Ego vs. Surfing in Religion

- Religion **as state ego** → authoritarian trap, brittle power.
- Religion **as surfing tradition** → humility, flow, empathy, pluralism.

☞ The key distinction: **Is faith used to silence Neutral and Opposite, or to enrich them?**

    •   Authoritarian rulers: God as a tool of Ego.
    •   Surfing wisdom: God as a reminder of humility, interdependence, and balance.

Surfing Wisdom Traditions (Expanded: Islamic Pathways)

Sufism: Mystical Surfing of the Soul

Sufism, the mystical tradition within Islam, emphasizes **inner transformation over external domination**. Where authoritarian interpretations of Islam enforce obedience to rulers, Sufism directs attention inward: ego (the *nafs*) must be disciplined, purified, and dissolved in love for the divine.

- **Ego Check (Your Position):**

The Sufi path begins by confronting the self's pride, anger, and desire. The self-centered ego is not destroyed but recognized as limited. This is surfing the most dangerous wave: the illusion of self as absolute.

- **Neutral Anchor (Facts of Impermanence):**

Sufism is grounded in a sober realism about life: wealth, status, even health are transient. This factual awareness keeps practitioners from clinging to illusions of permanence.

- **Opposite Voice (Universal Compassion):**

Sufi poets like Rumi and Hafiz insist on embracing the stranger, the outsider, even the enemy. Empathy is not a slogan but a mystical recognition: the divine exists in all.

Surfing Example: Rumi's lines — *"Out beyond ideas of wrongdoing and rightdoing there is a field. I'll meet you there."* — epitomize surfing wisdom. It doesn't deny wrong or right, but moves dynamically between them into a space of higher balance.

Lesson: Sufism shows how religion, often co-opted into ego-authoritarianism, can instead teach humility, empathy, and dynamic balance — a spiritual surfing that resists rigid dogma.

Andalusian Spain: A Civilizational Surfboard

Between the 8th and 15th centuries, **Al-Andalus** (Islamic Spain) became a crossroads of cultures: Muslim, Jewish, and Christian scholars translated texts, debated philosophy, and co-created knowledge. It was not utopia — conflicts existed — but it was one of history's most remarkable experiments in **surfing plurality**.

- **Ego (Islamic Rule):** Muslim rulers governed, often asserting dominance.

- **Neutral (Knowledge as Anchor):** Greek philosophy, Indian mathematics, and Persian medicine were translated into Arabic and Latin. Knowledge was shared across boundaries, becoming a Neutral platform.

- **Opposite (Plural Voices):** Jewish and Christian scholars were included in debates, synagogues and churches coexisted with mosques, and intellectual exchange was institutionalized.

Surfing Example:

The philosopher **Averroes (Ibn Rushd)** wrote extensive commentaries on Aristotle, later influencing Thomas Aquinas and shaping European thought. This was not one culture "winning," but a surfing exchange: Ego ambition (Islamic empire) riding Neutral data (Aristotle) and embracing Opposite voices (Jewish translators, Christian philosophers).

Lesson: Andalusian Spain demonstrates that civilizations thrive not by silencing others but by surfing diversity. When cultures welcome Neutral anchors (science, philosophy) and Opposite voices (other faiths, minorities), they unleash a wave of creativity that can transform the world.

Why These Traditions Matter Today

- **Against Religious Ego:** Sufism and Andalusia prove that Islam does not have to mean authoritarian hierarchy. The same tradition that gave us rigid clerical states also produced mysticism, pluralism, and Renaissance sparks.

- **For Surfing Culture:** These traditions embody the central thesis of surfing: **ego checked, facts honored, empathy included.**

- **Modern Implication:** In a world of polarization, citing Sufism and Andalusian Spain reminds us that civilizations already hold the seeds of surfing within their own histories. It is not "foreign" to balance, flow, and humility — it is deeply human.

Surfing Mandala: Culture & Philosophy
From Rigid Truths to Dynamic Wisdom

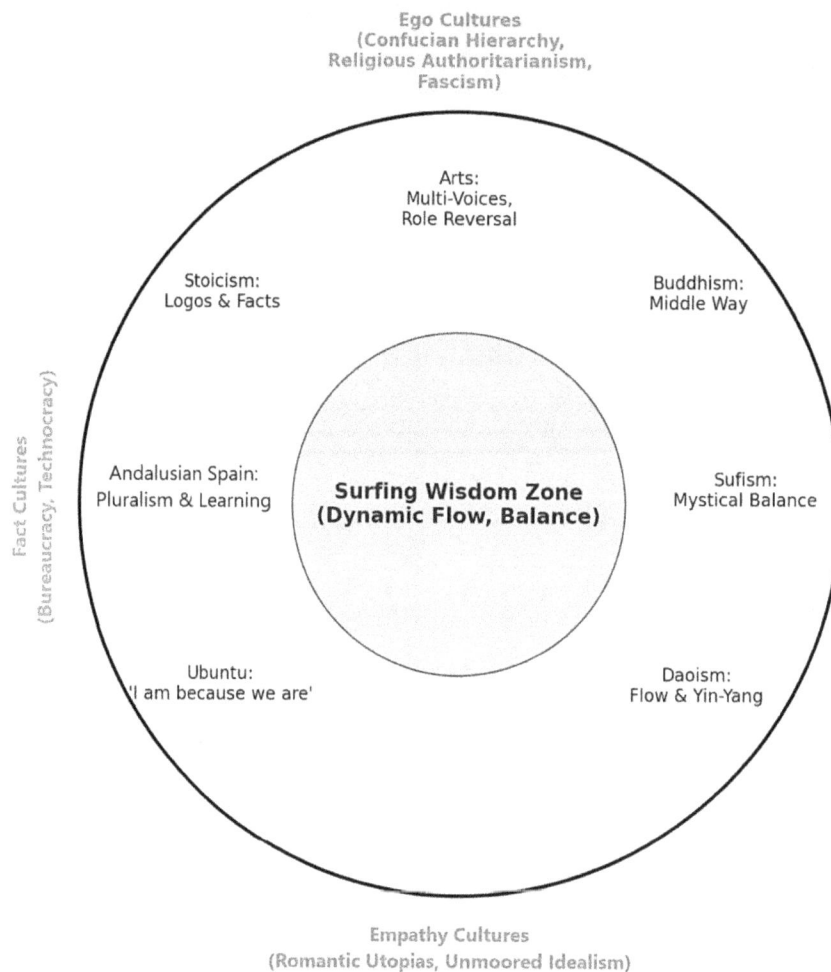

Ego Cultures
(Confucian Hierarchy,
Religious Authoritarianism,
Fascism)

Arts:
Multi-Voices,
Role Reversal

Stoicism:
Logos & Facts

Buddhism:
Middle Way

Fact Cultures
(Bureaucracy, Technocracy)

Andalusian Spain:
Pluralism & Learning

**Surfing Wisdom Zone
(Dynamic Flow, Balance)**

Sufism:
Mystical Balance

Ubuntu:
'I am because we are'

Daoism:
Flow & Yin-Yang

Empathy Cultures
(Romantic Utopias, Unmoored Idealism)

Surfing Mandala Diagram ◉ :

• **Ego Cultures (top, red):** now clarified as **Confucian hierarchy, religious authoritarianism, and fascism** — the three dominant patterns of rigid ego-driven systems.

• **Fact Cultures (left, green):** bureaucracy and technocracy.
• **Empathy Cultures (bottom, blue):** romantic utopias, unmoored idealism.

• **Center (gold zone):** Surfing Wisdom Zone, where traditions like Buddhism, Stoicism, Ubuntu, Daoism, and the Arts act as dynamic bridges.

Global Surf Map: Nations Riding Waves Toward Common Ground

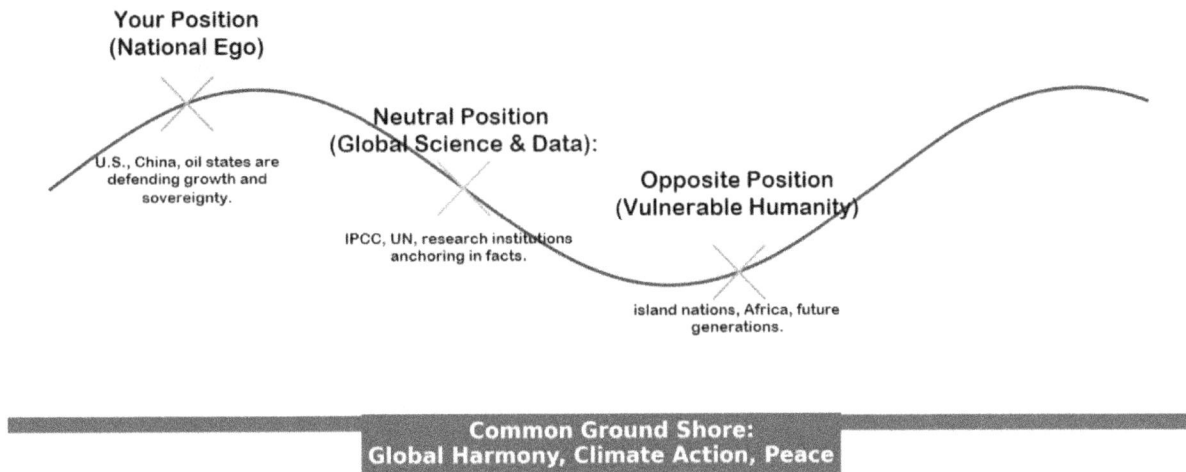

Your Position
(National Ego)

U.S., China, oil states are
defending growth and
sovereignty.

Neutral Position
(Global Science & Data):

IPCC, UN, research institutions
anchoring in facts.

Opposite Position
(Vulnerable Humanity)

island nations, Africa, future
generations.

Common Ground Shore:
Global Harmony, Climate Action, Peace

Global Surf Map Diagram 🌐 🌊

- **Your Position (National Ego):** U.S., China, oil states defending growth and sovereignty.
- **Neutral Position (Global Science & Data):** IPCC, UN, research institutions anchoring in facts.
- **Opposite Position (Vulnerable Humanity):** island nations, Africa, future generations.
- All ride the wave toward the **Common Ground Shore** — where climate action, global justice, and peace can converge.

Surfing Economy Diagram: Avoiding Traps, Finding Balance

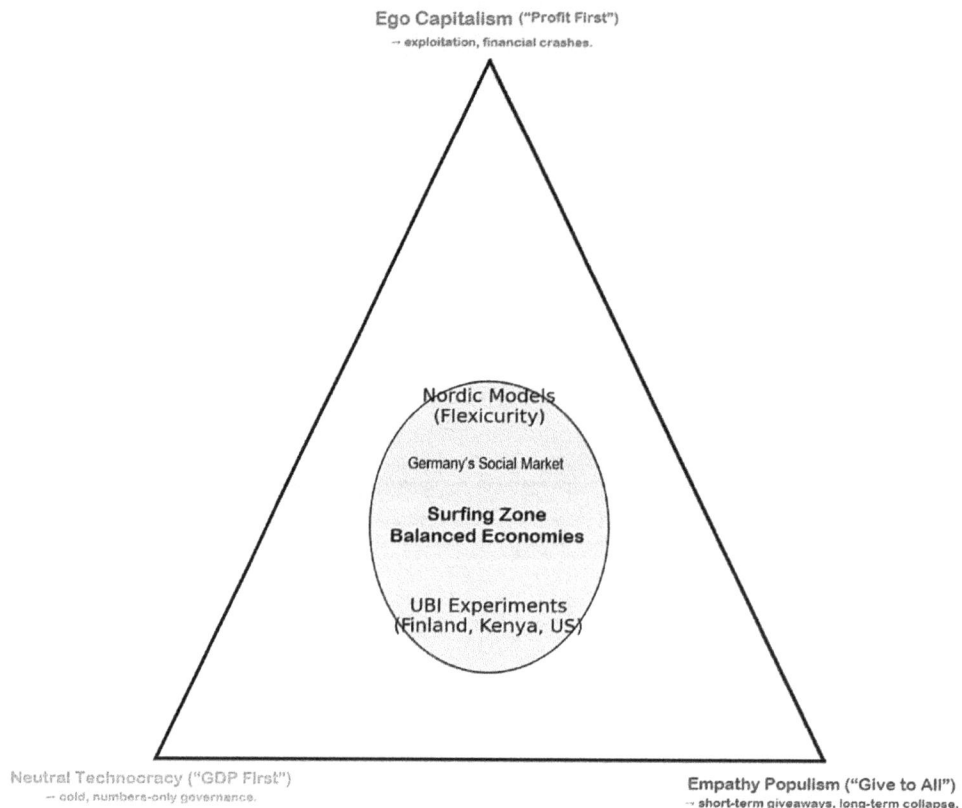

Ego Capitalism ("Profit First")
→ exploitation, financial crashes.

Nordic Models
(Flexicurity)

Germany's Social Market

**Surfing Zone
Balanced Economies**

UBI Experiments
(Finland, Kenya, US)

Neutral Technocracy ("GDP First")
→ cold, numbers-only governance.

Empathy Populism ("Give to All")
→ short-term giveaways, long-term collapse.

Surfing Economy Diagram 🏄 :

- **Triangle Corners (Traps):**

- 🔴 Ego Capitalism ("Profit First") → exploitation, financial crashes.
- ⚪ Neutral Technocracy ("GDP First") → cold, numbers-only governance.
- 🔴 Empathy Populism ("Give to All") → short-term giveaways, long-term collapse.

- **Center Gold Zone (Surfing Economies):**
- **Nordic Models (Flexicurity)** → innovation + welfare + trust.
- **Germany's Social Market** → postwar balance of capital & protection.
- **UBI Experiments** (Finland, Kenya, Stockton) → dignity baseline with data.

Chapter 8

The Future of Surfing Society: Embedding the Three Positions in Culture, Education, and Institutions

1. Introduction: From Individual Skill to Collective Culture

In previous chapters, we learned how surfing the Three Positions can transform **personal conflicts, leadership dilemmas, business negotiations, and even global crises**. But wisdom, when confined to a few individuals, is fragile.

History shows this clearly. A single leader like Mandela can surf, but what happens after he leaves? A visionary CEO may balance ego, facts, and empathy, but what about the company after succession? A family might practice surfing at home, but if children step into schools and media systems that reward tribalism, fear, or blind obedience, the practice dissolves.

This is why the next frontier is not **personal surfing**, but **collective surfing**.

- It must be **taught in schools** as naturally as mathematics.
- It must be **institutionalized** in courts, parliaments, and media standards.
- It must be **embedded in economies** so growth balances with dignity and justice.
- It must be **woven into culture and philosophy** so future generations see surfing as wisdom, not weakness.

In short: individuals can practice surfing, but only **Surfing Societies** can sustain it.

2. Education: Teaching Surfing to Children

2.1. Why Current Education Fails to Surf

Most education systems tilt toward one extreme:

- **Ego-dominant:** Competitive exams, rankings, and grades reinforce "Your Position." Students learn that success means beating others.
- **Neutral-only:** Facts are drilled, tests measure memory, but no space exists to discuss feelings or empathy.
- **Empathy-deficient:** Schools rarely ask children to imagine the world from another's perspective. Bullying often thrives because empathy is untrained.

As a result, adults graduate as **rigid thinkers**: either self-centered competitors, robotic technocrats, or naive idealists.

2.2. What Surfing Education Looks Like

Surfing education means students **practice all three positions daily**:

- **Role-play debates**: In history, one group defends colonizers, another defends colonized, then they switch sides.
- **Fact anchor exercises**: In science, students state personal beliefs about climate, then check against actual data.
- **Empathy storytelling**: In literature, students write diary entries from both the hero and villain's perspective.

Surfing classrooms grow children who are flexible, less dogmatic, and naturally more empathetic.

2.3. Case: Finland's Surfing Spirit

Finland revolutionized education by reducing rote memorization, extending teacher autonomy, and emphasizing collaboration. Students learn critical thinking and empathy through project-based tasks. It is no accident Finland ranks high not just in academics but in **life satisfaction**.

2.4. Daily Classroom Rituals

- **"Three Viewpoints Circle"**: At morning meetings, each child states their own opinion, one shared fact, and one imagined perspective of someone else.
- **"Conflict Surfing Rules"**: Arguments are paused until students state at least one Neutral fact and one Opposite empathy point.

☞ A surfing generation raised this way will be less polarized, more collaborative, and more humane.

3.3. Institutional Reform for Surfing

Institutions are not static monuments — they are **living surfboards**. They either keep societies afloat by balancing ego, facts, and empathy, or they collapse into weapons of domination. To make surfing durable, democracies and global systems must **reform themselves explicitly around the Three Positions model**.

Case 1: Citizen Assemblies in Ireland

Ireland provides a groundbreaking example of how a democracy can **surf its way through deeply divisive moral issues**.

- For decades, abortion and same-sex marriage were flashpoints. Traditional politics, stuck in **Your Position** (tribal party lines, religious ego), failed to produce progress.
- The government convened **citizen assemblies**, randomly selected groups of ordinary people.
- **Neutral Position:** Experts presented verified scientific, medical, and legal data.
- **Your Position:** Citizens voiced their own fears, traditions, and values.
- **Opposite Position:** Testimonies from women who had traveled abroad for abortions, or from LGBTQ citizens denied rights, brought the empathy dimension.

- The result was **surprising consensus** — reforms that politicians alone could not have achieved.
- Outcomes: Ireland legalized same-sex marriage in 2015 and repealed its abortion ban in 2018.

👉 Lesson: **Surfing assemblies** transform deadlock into dialogue by weaving data, ego, and empathy into one deliberative process.

Case 2: Truth & Reconciliation Commissions (South Africa)

When apartheid ended, South Africa faced an impossible wave: **decades of injustice, rage, and fear of civil war**.

- A purely **Your Position** approach (black majority seeking revenge) would have fueled violence.
- A purely **Neutral Position** approach (legal trials for all crimes) would have overwhelmed the courts and collapsed the state.
- A purely **Opposite Position** approach (blanket forgiveness) would have erased victims' dignity.

The **Truth and Reconciliation Commission (TRC)** became a pioneering institutional surfer:
- **Neutral:** Rigorous fact-finding, documentation of crimes, hearings across the nation.
- **Opposite:** Victims gave testimony — their pain was recognized publicly, validating dignity.
- **Your:** The state preserved sovereignty and stability by granting conditional amnesty.

It was not perfect. Some perpetrators escaped full accountability; many victims felt justice incomplete. But as an institutional surfboard, the TRC prevented a spiral into vengeance and gave South Africa a path toward fragile peace.

Lesson: Surfing institutions are not flawless. But they **manage conflict in motion**, preventing collapse.

Case 3: Deliberative Polling (U.S. and Taiwan)

Political scientist James Fishkin pioneered **deliberative polling**, where citizens are gathered, given **balanced information**, and then surveyed again after discussion.

- In the U.S., this method softened polarization on issues like healthcare.
- In Taiwan, deliberative forums have been used to build consensus on energy policy, where facts (Neutral), party lines (Your), and local community concerns (Opposite) were all heard.

Lesson: Surfing reforms can **stabilize even polarized democracies**, if they create structured space for perspective-taking.

Case 4: Germany's "Concertation" Model

In post-war Germany, economic policy was often negotiated through "concertation" — tripartite councils of government, business, and labor unions.

- Business defended **Your Position** (profit, competitiveness).
- Economists anchored **Neutral** (inflation, productivity data).
- Unions voiced **Opposite** (workers' wages, dignity).

Together, they forged policies like the social market economy, which became a foundation of Germany's prosperity.

Lesson: Embedding all three positions into **policy-making institutions** creates resilience across decades.

Surfing Reform Blueprint

1.   **Parliaments:** Require three-position debates before major laws. Every bill must include (a) constituency interests (Your), (b) independent fact reports (Neutral), and (c) testimony from affected minorities (Opposite).

2.   **Courts:** Expand beyond technical rulings by introducing empathy hearings, where victims or vulnerable groups testify before constitutional decisions.

3.   **Councils & Committees:** Adopt the citizen assembly model, especially for divisive issues like climate, healthcare, or bioethics.

4.   **Global Institutions:** The UN could embed surfing by mandating fact panels (IPCC), sovereignty defenses (states' Your), and vulnerable voices (small nations, future generations) in all climate or security debates.

👉 Democracies will not survive the 21st century if they remain ego arenas or technocratic silos. They must **adopt surfing mechanisms in parliaments, courts, and councils** to evolve into institutions of balance, not battlefields of polarization.

4. Media & Information: From Polarization to Surfing Platforms

4.1. Media as Surfing Gatekeeper

The media is not just another institution; it is the **lens through which reality is constructed**. For most citizens, reality is not experienced directly but mediated by news, social feeds, and screens. This makes media the most powerful surfboard of all — it determines whether societies balance ego, facts, and empathy, or collapse into distortion.

Today's landscape is broken:

• **Ego amplification:** Social media algorithms prioritize outrage. Rage and tribalism go viral faster than nuance. This locks audiences into **Your Position** echo chambers.

• **Neutral suppression:** Independent journalists who anchor facts are labeled "biased" or "fake news" by regimes or partisans. Truth itself becomes suspect.

• **Empathy weaponized:** Populist leaders manipulate compassion — "Think of our people" — while ignoring data or silencing others' suffering. This creates empathy without balance, empathy as propaganda.

☞ When media stops surfing, societies drown in polarization.

4.2. Surfing Media Standards

What would a **surfing media ecosystem** look like? It requires rules and practices that force the three positions to appear together:

1. **Triple Perspective Reporting:** Every story must include:

• **Your Position** → the ego-driven or interest-based side (what government, elites, or groups want).

• **Neutral Position** → verified facts, data, and evidence.

• **Opposite Position** → voices of those marginalized, harmed, or left out.

Labeling: News stories should **explicitly flag** which perspective is being presented. Imagine TV graphics:

- • ⬤ *Your Position*
- • ⬤ *Neutral Facts*
- • ⬤ *Opposite Voices*

2. **Rotation of Journalists:** Reporters should be periodically rotated across beats and perspectives to prevent them from sinking into one echo chamber.

4. **Fact Anchoring:** Stories must cite independent, verifiable sources before they are published. Platforms should provide sidebars linking to fact-checking agencies.

👉 This could evolve into **Surfing Media Charters** — professional standards enforced by journalism associations, much like existing codes of ethics.

4.3. Case Studies: Media in Motion

- • **BBC / NPR:** Both attempt to balance, often presenting multiple perspectives. Ironically, being attacked by both left and right is evidence they attempt to surf.

- • **Fox News, RT, Global Times:** Collapse into **ego propaganda**, serving one power bloc. They abandon Neutral and Opposite entirely.

- • **Constructive Journalism / Solutions Journalism:** Emerging models where outlets not only report problems but include empathy (human stories) and Neutral (policy evidence). This is closer to surfing.

4.4. Solidarity Journalism: Beyond Neutrality

Some scholars and activists argue that media should not only "balance" but show **solidarity with truth and justice**. This means:

- Not treating lies and facts as equal.
- Not giving platforms to ego-driven propaganda in the name of "fairness."
- Aligning with the **Neutral Position** (truth) while still including empathy and opposing perspectives.

👉 Solidarity is not bias — it is **anchored empathy with accountability**. It says: *we will hear all voices, but we will not equate falsehood with truth.*

4.5. The Role of Citizens: How to Surf News Daily

Institutions alone cannot save us. Citizens must learn to be **everyday surfers of information**. Here are practical steps:

1. **Fact-Check Habit:**
   - Use trusted fact-checkers (AP Fact Check, Snopes, Full Fact).
   - Cross-verify a story in at least 2–3 outlets with different leanings.

2. **Surf Across Perspectives:**

   - For every news story, ask:
   - What is **Your Position** (whose ego or interest is served)?
   - What is **Neutral** (what facts are cited)?
   - What is **Opposite** (who is left out or harmed)?

3. **Spot Emotional Manipulation:**

   - If a headline makes you instantly angry, pause. Is this outrage clickbait? Which position is being exaggerated?

4. **Practice Media Solidarity:**

- Support outlets that at least attempt to surf.
- Pay subscriptions where possible — free journalism is often funded by clicks, which incentivizes ego and outrage.

5. **Family Media Surfing Rituals:**

- Discuss news at dinner: each person states (a) whose ego is in play, (b) what facts anchor the story, (c) what empathy voices are missing.
- This makes surfing a civic habit at home.

4.6. Conclusion: Media as the Ocean of Democracy

Media is the ocean we swim in every day. If the waters are polluted by ego, lies, or propaganda, even the best leaders drown. If they are cleaned and surfed — balancing self-interest, truth, and empathy — then democracy breathes again.

The **right thing to do**, as both institutions and individuals, is not blind neutrality or blind solidarity, but **surfing solidarity**:

- Anchored in fact.
- Open to empathy.
- Conscious of ego.

☞ Only then can news serve what it was meant to: not to divide us, but to carry us, wave by wave, toward a common shore of reality, trust, and solidarity.

5. Economy: Surfing Capitalism and Equality

5.1. The Three Economic Traps

Economic systems, like individuals, often fall into one-dimensional traps:

1. **Ego Capitalism — "Profit First."**
   • The pure neoliberal model that triumphed in the 1980s–2000s. Deregulation, privatization, shareholder supremacy.
   • Short-term growth achieved, but at enormous costs: worker exploitation, environmental collapse, financial bubbles.
   • Example: the 2008 financial crisis, where Wall Street's ego-driven pursuit of profit collapsed global markets and left millions jobless.

2. **Neutral Technocracy — "GDP First."**

   • Governments obsessed with statistics: growth rates, inflation targets, fiscal deficits.
   • In this trap, policy becomes cold, ignoring human dignity. Citizens are reduced to numbers.
   • Example: austerity policies in Greece post-2010, where Neutral technocrats demanded balanced budgets while ordinary people lost jobs, homes, and hope.

3. **Empathy Populism — "Give to All."**

   • Politicians seeking quick popularity hand out subsidies, cash, or free goods without sustainable data.
   • Short-term relief feels good, but economies collapse under debt or inflation.
   • Example: Venezuela's oil-fueled populism. The government promised cheap fuel, free goods, and massive subsidies, but ignored Neutral economic data. When oil prices fell, the system imploded, leaving citizens starving.

   ☞ None of these traps sustain societies. A surfing economy requires **balancing all three**: ego (innovation, profit), Neutral (data, sustainability), and Opposite (workers, poor, vulnerable).

5.2. Surfing Economies: Models in Practice

Germany's Social Market Model

Post–World War II, Germany faced ruin. It needed growth but also stability. The "Soziale Marktwirtschaft" (Social Market Economy) became a **surfing system**:

- **Your Position (Ego):** Businesses retained freedom to innovate and compete globally.

- **Neutral (Data):** Economic councils monitored inflation, productivity, exports. Policy was data-driven.

- **Opposite (Empathy):** Strong worker protections, co-determination (workers on corporate boards), generous social insurance.

The result? Germany became Europe's economic engine while maintaining relatively high equality and worker dignity.

   Lesson: Surfing is not compromise. It is structural design — institutions that weave all three positions into law.

Nordic Economies: High Trust Surfers

The Nordic countries (Sweden, Denmark, Norway, Finland, Iceland) are often misunderstood. Outsiders caricature them as "socialist utopias." In reality, they are **hyper-capitalist surfers**.

- **Ego (Innovation & Markets):**
- Nordic economies are among the most competitive in the world. Sweden birthed Spotify, Klarna, Ericsson. Denmark has Lego, Novo Nordisk. Finland produced Nokia and gaming giants like Supercell.
- Labor markets are flexible: it is relatively easy for companies to hire and fire. Ego energy thrives.
- **Neutral (Data & Policy):**

- Nordic governance is technocratic but transparent. Policies are evidence-based, informed by expert commissions.
- Economic stability is carefully monitored: balanced budgets, competitive tax incentives for innovation.
- **Opposite (Empathy & Welfare):**
- Universal healthcare, free education, generous parental leave, unemployment insurance.
- High taxes (sometimes 45–55% of income) fund a **solidarity system** — but citizens accept it because trust is high: corruption is low, money is transparently reinvested.

Key to Nordic Surfing:

- **High social trust.** Citizens believe taxes are used fairly.
- **Flexicurity model.** Companies get flexibility (ego), workers get security (opposite), governments anchor it with Neutral data.
- **Equality as productivity.** By ensuring everyone has education and healthcare, societies unleash innovation from the widest pool of talent.

☞ This is perhaps the clearest **civilization-scale example of surfing economies**.

UBI (Universal Basic Income) Experiments

UBI is a modern attempt to surf inequality by providing **dignity as a baseline**.

- **Finland (2017–2019):**
- 2,000 unemployed people received €560/month, no strings attached.
- Neutral economists tracked results.
- Findings: recipients reported less stress, more happiness, and were slightly more likely to find work.

- Empathy was honored without destroying Neutral economic discipline.
- **Kenya (GiveDirectly, ongoing):**
- Villages receive unconditional cash transfers, sometimes for over a decade.
- Neutral evaluation shows improved nutrition, investment in small businesses, and long-term empowerment.
- No evidence of laziness; in fact, communities became more resilient.
- **U.S. (Stockton, California, 2019–2021):**
- 125 low-income residents received $500/month.
- Neutral analysis: recipients were twice as likely to find full-time jobs as non-recipients. Stress declined, health improved.
- Shows that UBI is not charity, but a **surfing mechanism**: ego (work motivation), Neutral (data), and Opposite (human dignity) aligned.

👉 Critics warn of costs, but the evidence so far shows that **giving dignity first** unleashes creativity and stability — a classic surfing effect.

🔄 5.3. Corporate Surfing

Future corporations must surf the same Three Positions as societies:

- **Ego (Your Position):** Deliver innovation and profits.
- **Neutral (Facts):** Operate with transparent, verifiable data.
- **Opposite (Empathy):** Respect workers, communities, and the planet.

Better Case Studies:

1. **Patagonia (Outdoor Apparel)**
   - Ego: Remains profitable with loyal customers worldwide.
   - Neutral: Transparent supply chain audits, carbon data reports.

- Opposite: "Earth is our only shareholder" — profits legally placed into environmental trust.

☞ True surfing: ego, fact, and empathy embedded into governance.

2. Novo Nordisk (Pharma, Denmark)

- Ego: Leading producer of diabetes treatments, highly profitable.
- Neutral: Transparent R&D investment, clinical trial data shared.
- Opposite: Global access programs → provides insulin at reduced costs in low-income nations.

☞ Example of Nordic surfing ethos applied to a global company.

3. Interface (Carpet & Flooring, USA)

- Ego: Stayed competitive in a low-margin industry.
- Neutral: Pioneered "Mission Zero," a data-anchored goal of zero environmental impact by 2020.
- Opposite: Products redesigned for recyclability; employees and communities engaged in purpose-driven mission.

☞ Shows that industrial firms, not just trendy brands, can surf profit + data + empathy.

4. Mondragon Corporation (Worker Cooperative, Spain)

- Ego: Over 80,000 employees across industries, sustainable business performance.
- Neutral: Annual reports and cooperative accountability mechanisms.
- Opposite: Worker ownership model → wages capped so CEOs don't earn more than ~6x average worker pay.

☞ A structural surfboard: ego (business survival), neutral (data-driven co-op governance), opposite (worker dignity) in one.

✖ Why Microsoft & Unilever Are Weak Surfers

- **Microsoft:** Yes, it has AI ethics councils — but they lack binding power. Ego (market dominance) outweighs Neutral or Opposite. Example: layoffs contradict philanthropic messaging.
- **Unilever:** Publicly promotes sustainability, but many ESG claims are shallow or unverified ("greenwashing"). True surfing requires **accountability**, not just marketing.

5.4. Conclusion: Civilizing Capitalism

Surfing economies do not reject capitalism. They **civilize it**.

- Ego drives innovation and growth.
- Neutral keeps systems honest and efficient.
- Opposite ensures dignity, justice, and social trust.

Germany's social market, the Nordics' flexicurity, and UBI experiments all prove that **surfing is possible**. By contrast, Venezuela's collapse and Wall Street's crises show what happens when surfing fails.

The future economy must be built as a **surfboard system**: flexible, data-anchored, and compassionate — or else it will collapse under the weight of ego, blind technocracy, or unsustainable populism.

6. Governance: Surfing Democracies and Global Councils (Expanded)

6.1. Democracies in Crisis: How Ego Polarization Breaks the System

Diagnosis. Modern democracies are captured by **Your Position** dynamics: party identity over public interest, tribal media ecosystems, and "base-only" tactics. The result is gridlock at home and incoherence abroad.

Contemporary pressure points

1. **Tariffs/duties & weaponized trade (U.S. and beyond).**

- **Ego pattern:** "Protect *our* jobs from 'unfair' others." Tariffs are announced as political signals; exemptions become bargaining chips; retaliation cycles escalate.
- **Neutral gap:** Absent or selectively used cost-benefit analysis on downstream consumers, supply-chain inflation, retaliation risks, and security trade-offs.
- **Opposite blind spot:** Allies, smaller exporters, and domestic small businesses that depend on imported inputs are rarely given voice.
- **Systemic risk:** Tit-for-tat duties harden blocs, undermine rules-based trade, and invite **policy drift**: economic policy driven by election calendars, not evidence.

2. **Constitutional hardball (U.S., Israel, parts of EU).**

- **Ego pattern:** "Win first, justify later." Court-packing threats, emergency decrees, or rule changes for short-term gain.
- **Neutral gap:** Weakening of independent budget offices, statistics agencies, or judicial review.
- **Opposite blind spot:** Minorities' future rights and the losing side's long-term trust.

3. **Referendum populism (Brexit as archetype).**

- **Ego pattern:** Reduce complex policy to a single emotive slogan.
- **Neutral gap:** Insufficient, independent impact assessments; misinformation outpaces corrections.
- **Opposite blind spot:** Regions, sectors, or generations that bear heavier transition costs.

4. **Platform-driven outrage cycles (many democracies).**

- **Ego pattern:** Micro-targeted fear, "owning" the other side.
- **Neutral gap:** Algorithms optimize for engagement, not truth.

- **Opposite blind spot:** The out-group is caricatured, not heard.

Why it fails (mechanics):

- **Policy volatility** → business under-invests, allies hedge, adversaries probe.
- **Legitimacy erosion** → even good policies face non-compliance.
- **Crisis fragility** → when shocks hit (pandemic, war, financial), the system lacks shared facts and mutual trust.

6.2. The Illusion of Authoritarian "Surfing"

Authoritarians claim they can balance growth, order, and welfare (**they pretend to surf**). In reality:

- **Your Position dominates:** Power is centralized; loyalty beats competence.
- **Neutral is neutered:** Statistics, courts, and audits are politicized; truth becomes elastic.
- **Opposite is silenced:** Civil society, minorities, and critics are excluded or criminalized.

Short-term mirage, long-term math:

- Near-term "stability" is often debt-fueled or repression-enforced.
- **Unseen risks build**: misallocated capital, brittle supply chains, falsified safety/health data.
- **Crisis outcomes are worse** because systems can't self-correct: whistleblowers fear, media can't warn, courts can't constrain.

Takeaway: Authoritarianism mimics surfing rhetoric ("for the people," "scientific governance"), but structurally it is **ego with propaganda**. It cannot pass the Three Positions audit.

6.3. Surfing Democracies: Architecture, Guardrails, and Metrics

To surf sustainably, democracies need **institutionalized checks** that force leaders and parties to cycle through **Ego → Neutral → Opposite** before acting.

A. Structural Guardrails (what to build or strengthen)

1. **Representation (Your Position, safely channeled)**
   - **Open primaries / ranked-choice voting**: reduce base capture; reward cross-coalition appeal.
   - **Redistricting by independent commissions**: curb gerrymanders that radicalize incentives.
   - **Public financing / ad transparency**: dilute narrow-donor capture of agendas.

2. **Independent Truth Anchors (Neutral Position)**

   - **Statistical independence by law** (inflation, poverty, labor market, climate data).
   - **Nonpartisan budget & impact offices** (publish costs of tariffs, tax changes, defense plans).
   - **Science & ethics councils** with subpoena power for public health, AI/biotech, cyber.
   - **Algorithmic transparency** mandates for large platforms (auditable risk reports).

3. **Institutionalized Empathy (Opposite Position)**

   - **Minority rights entrenched in constitutional law** (hard to amend).
   - **Empathy hearings** in legislatures: affected communities testify **before** votes.
   - **Citizen assemblies** for divisive issues (random selection + expert briefings + testimony).
   - **Impact equity clauses**: require distributional analyses (by income/region/generation).

B. Policy Process—Surfing Protocol (how to decide)

Before major actions (tariffs, security acts, emergency powers):

1. **Your Position brief (max 2 pages):** Legitimate national/constituency interests and risks if unmet.

2. **Neutral Assessment (independent):** Quantified impacts (prices, jobs, allies, retaliation), scenario ranges, assumptions.

3. **Opposite Docket:**

   - **Domestic:** SMEs using imported inputs, consumers, minority regions.
   - **External:** Allies' trade/security positions, small exporters, humanitarian implications.

4. **Synthesis Memo:** Options A–C, trade-offs, mitigations (e.g., targeted relief vs. broad tariffs).

5. **Sunset + Review:** Automatic expiry unless performance metrics are met; publish ex-post evaluation.

B. Indicators & Early Warnings (are we surfing or sliding?)

- **Ego spike:** Rhetoric escalates (blame, purity tests), emergency shortcuts become routine, data agencies undermined.
- **Neutral decay:** Fewer independent reports accompany bills; forecasting and audits shrink; "security" claims replace numbers.
- **Opposite silenced:** Hearings shorten or disappear; civic groups excluded; protest framed as treason.
- **Outcome volatility:** Policy U-turns post-election; allies reduce intelligence/trade cooperation; credit downgrades, investment delays.

Target state ("Surfing Signals"):

- Cross-party amendments pass on key files.

- Impact notes precede votes; ex-post reviews trigger course corrections.
- Minority/region testimonies visible in final bill justifications.
- International coordination statements cite **both** national interest **and** shared evidence.

6.4. Global Surf Councils: From Ad-hoc Coalitions to Evidence-Led Compacts

Great-power rivalry and economic fragmentation make **rules-based cooperation** hard—but not impossible. A **Global Surf Charter** would formalize the Three Positions across key domains.

A. Climate–Energy Council (permanent)
- **Your Position:** National energy security, jobs, industrial base.
- **Neutral:** Carbon budgets, tech costs, grid constraints, border-adjustment math.
- **Opposite:** Vulnerable states (islands, least-developed countries), inter-generational impacts.

Protocols:

- **Transition deals**: green-tech access + financing in exchange for phased coal exits.
- **Carbon border adjustments** tied to verifiable data to avoid tariff wars.
- **Crisis clause**: fast-track coordination for supply shocks (e.g., war, drought).

B Trade & Supply-Chain Council

- **Your Position:** Domestic industry resilience; critical tech & health security.
- **Neutral:** Input–output modeling (price pass-through, capacity), retaliation likelihood, WTO compatibility.
- **Opposite:** SMEs, consumer groups, low-income exporters.

Protocols:

- **Pre-tariff stress tests** + targeted, time-limited measures with relief for downstream users.
- **Friend-shoring compacts** that publish costs & timelines; avoid "announce-only" politics.
- **Joint early-warning system** for shortages (chips, medicines, fertilizers).

C. Digital & AI Norms Council

- **Your Position:** Innovation leadership, national security.
- **Neutral:** Safety test suites, bias/robustness metrics, compute governance.
- **Opposite:** Civil liberties groups, labor, educators, children's advocates.

Protocols:

- **Risk-tiered regulation** + auditability; international red-lines (e.g., mass biometric surveillance in public).
- **Compute transparency** exchange among trusted partners; incident reporting.

D. Conflict & Civilians Forum

- **Your Position:** Security doctrines, deterrence needs.
- **Neutral:** Law of armed conflict, verified casualty methods, humanitarian access.
- **Opposite:** Civilians' testimony, neutral NGOs.

Protocols:

- **Civilians-first triggers**: ceasefire corridors when thresholds crossed.
- **After-action transparency**: public assessments, reparations pathways.

Why it works: Surf Councils don't demand kumbaya. They **force** ego to meet evidence and empathy **in the same room**, raising the political cost of performative posturing and lowering the cost of reasonable compromise.

Application to Today's "Duty/Tariff Threat" Waves (including U.S.)

Ego-only approach:

- Blanket tariffs framed as fairness/national pride; limited analysis; retaliation brushed aside.
- Domestic winners (few) visible; **domestic losers (many)**—import-dependent SMEs, consumers—ignored.
- Allies blindsided → coalitions fray; rivals exploit splits.

Surfing alternative (playbook):

1. **Neutral first:** Independent price/job modeling (who pays, how much, when). Publish ranges.
2. **Opposite second:** Hearings with SMEs, retailers, low-income consumer reps, allied trade partners.
3. **Your consolidated:** National security cases (narrowly defined) + targeted relief/transition for exposed sectors.
4. **Design choices:**
   - Prefer **narrow, time-bound, reviewable** measures over blanket tariffs.
   - Pair with **domestic mitigation** (tax credits for consumers or input rebates for SMEs).
   - **Coordinate** with allies to reduce leakage and geopolitical blowback.
5. **Sunset + scorecards:** If objectives (jobs, reshoring, resilience) aren't met by review dates, measures lapse or pivot.

Benefits: You still protect legitimate interests, but you **avoid self-harm** and **preserve alliances**—critical in an era of system-level rivalry.

Executive Playbooks & Checklists

A) Pre-Action Surfing Checklist (for any big move: tariffs, emergency powers, security bill)

- Have we written a 1-page **Your Position** memo (interests & risks)?
- Do we have an **independent Neutral** impact note (costs, scenarios, assumptions)?
- Have we held **Opposite/Empathy hearings** (domestic losers, allies, future generations)?
- Is there a **narrower, time-limited** option with mitigation?
- Are **sunset & review** clauses attached with public scorecards?
- Have we coordinated with **trusted partners** to reduce blowback?

B) Domestic Health Metrics (watch after enactment)

- Policy stability (amendments vs. U-turns)
- Compliance & litigation rates
- Public trust indices (esp. among losers)
- Investment & hiring trends in targeted sectors
- Ally coordination statements (trade, security)

C) Citizen's Surfing Guide to Government News

- **Your:** Who gains power/money/status from this policy?
- **Neutral:** Where is the independent impact note? If none, why?
- **Opposite:** Who pays (consumers, small firms, regions, future taxpayers)?
- **Test:** Is there a sunset/review? Are allies onboard? What's the plan if costs bite?

Bottom Line

- **Ego-only democracy** (tariffs as theater, emergency powers as default, base-feeding rhetoric) **wins the news cycle and loses the decade**—economically, institutionally, and strategically.
- **Authoritarian "stability"** is merely **ego plus propaganda**; it fails the Three Positions audit and breaks when shocks come.
- **Surfing governance** is harder upfront—but cheaper and safer over time. It **channels Your Position** into legitimate representation, **binds decisions to Neutral** evidence, and **institutionalizes Opposite** empathy through hearings, assemblies, and rights.
- **Global Surf Councils** turn zero-sum rivalry into constrained competition with rules, metrics, and crisis playbooks.

In one sentence:

The antidote to tribal collapse at home and authoritarian illusion abroad is **institutionalized surfing**—a governance design that forces ego to meet evidence and empathy before power moves.

7. Culture & Philosophy: From Rigid Truths to Surfing Wisdom

7.1. The Cultural Traps: How Societies Freeze in One Position

Surfing is dynamic; cultures often fossilize. The most dangerous traps are when entire civilizations orient themselves around a single position and call it "truth."

Ego Cultures (Hierarchies & Nationalism/Religious Absolutism)
- In these societies, identity is defined by obedience: to rulers, ancestors, or religious authority. "Your Position" becomes a collective ego, inflating itself against all others.

- **Examples:**

- **Confucian authoritarianism in China**: hierarchy, filial loyalty, and state-centered morality.
- **Authoritarian political Islam**: regimes where religious authority dominates governance, rejecting pluralism and democratic checks.
- **20th-century fascism**: worship of nation and leader, suppression of dissent.
- **Why it fails:** Ego cultures generate energy and cohesion, but they cannot self-correct. Dissent = betrayal, so mistakes snowball into catastrophe (wars, repression, economic collapse).

• Fact Cultures (Bureaucracy & Technocracy).

- These civilizations elevate "Neutral" numbers, rules, and procedures into ultimate values.
- **Examples:** The Soviet bureaucracy, Weberian bureaucratic empires, corporate technocracies.
- **Why it fails:** They suffocate vitality. Human beings become case files, statistics, "inputs." Eventually, creativity and empathy drain away, leaving brittle shells that shatter under crisis.
- **Empathy Cultures (Romantic Idealism).**
- Societies fall in love with ideals of compassion, harmony, or utopia, but without Neutral anchors.
- **Examples:** Some 19th-century utopian communes, Venezuela's populist promises, religious cults preaching love but ignoring power realities.
- **Why it fails:** Without data and limits, empathy cultures overspend, overpromise, and implode. Love is real, but it cannot balance books or repel armies.

☞ These traps show that **culture is not only art or ritual — it is the invisible gravity that can either drown societies in one-sided truths or allow them to surf.**

Case extended : Religious Authoritarianism in Islamic Contexts)

Ego cultures emerge wherever authority is absolute, dissent is equated with betrayal, and identity is enforced as loyalty. While Confucian hierarchy and fascist nationalism are classic forms, another enduring type is **religious authoritarian governance** in parts of the Islamic world.

A. Religious Authoritarianism: Faith as Political Ego

- **When religion is fused with state power**, faith ceases to be a personal or communal path and becomes an instrument of political control.
- Leaders or clerics claim to embody divine will; therefore, opposing them equals opposing God.
- Neutral data (economics, science, human rights law) is dismissed as "Western" or "corrupted."
- Opposite voices (minorities, women, dissidents, secular citizens) are silenced under charges of heresy or blasphemy.

Examples in practice:

- **Iran (post-1979):** Supreme Leader claims ultimate authority, making all other institutions subordinate. Ego: clerical rule. Neutral: economic mismanagement hidden. Opposite: women, minorities, protesters suppressed.
- **Taliban's Afghanistan:** Religious purity overruled Neutral (schooling, economic data) and Opposite (women's rights, ethnic groups). The result: long-term instability.
- **Saudi Arabia's Wahhabi tradition (20th century):** Religious police enforced rigid moral codes; dissent crushed. Recently, partial reforms introduced Neutral pragmatism, but Ego remains dominant.

Why it fails:
- **Rigidity**: When divine will is monopolized by rulers, no correction is possible without theological rebellion.
- **Blindness**: Neutral evidence is ignored; data on health, economy, climate, and education are censored if inconvenient.

- **Exclusion**: Empathy is restricted to "the faithful," leaving others invisible.

Thus, like nationalism or Confucian hierarchy, religious authoritarianism is an **ego culture**: powerful, cohesive, but brittle and self-destructive.

B. Surfing Potentials Inside Islamic Civilization

It is crucial not to equate Islam itself with authoritarian ego. **Within Islamic history and philosophy, powerful surfing traditions exist** that point toward balance.

1. **Sufism (Mystical Islam).**
   - Focuses on humility, self-emptying, and union with the divine.
   - Surfing resonance: Ego (self-centeredness) is deconstructed, Neutral (facts of impermanence) is embraced, Opposite (love for all beings) is institutionalized in poetry, rituals, and service.
   - Rumi's poetry: *"Out beyond ideas of wrongdoing and rightdoing there is a field. I'll meet you there."* — a surfing vision of common ground.

2. **Andalusian Spain (8th–15th centuries).**
   - In medieval Córdoba and Granada, Muslim, Christian, and Jewish scholars coexisted and co-created.
   - Surfing in practice: Ego (Islamic rule) balanced with Neutral (Greek-Arabic science, philosophy) and Opposite (plural communities).
   - This produced breakthroughs in medicine, astronomy, and philosophy, later fueling the European Renaissance.

3. **Modern Islamic Surfing Efforts.**
   - Indonesia: Though imperfect, its democracy integrates Islamic values with pluralist governance.
   - Tunisia's Arab Spring: The most successful early experiment in balancing religious identity with democratic Neutral anchors and Opposite protections for women.

C. Lessons: Ego vs. Surfing in Religion
- Religion **as state ego** → authoritarian trap, brittle power.
- Religion **as surfing tradition** → humility, flow, empathy, pluralism.

The key distinction: **Is faith used to silence Neutral and Opposite, or to enrich them?**
- Authoritarian rulers: God as a tool of Ego.
- Surfing wisdom: God as a reminder of humility, interdependence, and balance.

7.2. Surfing Wisdom Traditions: Philosophical Roots Without Dogma

Surfing may sound modern, but the **intuition that wisdom lies beyond extremes** has deep roots across cultures.
- **Buddhism (The Middle Way).**
- Siddhartha Gautama rejected both indulgence and extreme asceticism.
- The "Middle Way" is not compromise, but a dynamic awareness of how craving and denial both trap the self.
- Surfing resonates: the surfer doesn't kill the wave (ego) or drown under it (empathy), but rides it with mindful awareness.
- ⚠ But caution: Buddhism's compassion can be misinterpreted as passive tolerance of injustice. Surfing requires active balance, not withdrawal.
- **Stoicism (Ancient Greece & Rome).**
- Anchored in facts (logos) and self-control, Stoicism urged living "according to nature" and not being enslaved by passions.
- In surfing terms: Stoicism strengthens the Neutral anchor. It protects against Ego rage and Empathy overwhelm.
- Marcus Aurelius wrote: "If you are distressed by anything external, the pain is not due to the thing itself but your estimate of it." A classic Neutral reframe.
- **Ubuntu (Sub-Saharan Africa).**

- Philosophy of "I am because we are."
- Anchors empathy at the social level: personhood is realized through relationships.
- In surfing terms: Ubuntu prevents Ego hyper-individualism. It ensures the Opposite voice (the marginalized) remains inside the circle of humanity.
- **Daoism (China).**
- "The Dao that can be spoken is not the eternal Dao." Daoism honors flow, paradox, and balance.
- Yin–yang is a proto-surfing metaphor: opposites exist in each other, and wisdom is riding the flow rather than forcing rigid control.
- **Indigenous Knowledge Systems.**
- Many First Nations and Indigenous traditions understand harmony as *dynamic reciprocity* with land, animals, and ancestors.
- This is surfing writ ecological: Ego (use of resources), Neutral (seasonal/factual knowledge), Opposite (future generations, non-human voices).

But key difference: Surfing is not passive "balance" or rigid "harmony." It is **dynamic flow under pressure**. A surfer leans left or right because the wave demands it, not because symmetry looks nice. That flexibility is what rigid philosophies often miss.

Surfing Wisdom Traditions (Expanded: Islamic Pathways)

Sufism: Mystical Surfing of the Soul

Sufism, the mystical tradition within Islam, emphasizes **inner transformation over external domination**. Where authoritarian interpretations of Islam enforce obedience to rulers, Sufism directs attention inward: ego (the *nafs*) must be disciplined, purified, and dissolved in love for the divine.

- **Ego Check (Your Position):**

The Sufi path begins by confronting the self's pride, anger, and desire. The self-centered ego is not destroyed but recognized as limited. This is surfing the most dangerous wave: the illusion of self as absolute.

- **Neutral Anchor (Facts of Impermanence):**
Sufism is grounded in a sober realism about life: wealth, status, even health are transient. This factual awareness keeps practitioners from clinging to illusions of permanence.

- **Opposite Voice (Universal Compassion):**
Sufi poets like Rumi and Hafiz insist on embracing the stranger, the outsider, even the enemy. Empathy is not a slogan but a mystical recognition: the divine exists in all.

Surfing Example: Rumi's lines — *"Out beyond ideas of wrongdoing and rightdoing there is a field. I'll meet you there."* — epitomize surfing wisdom. It doesn't deny wrong or right, but moves dynamically between them into a space of higher balance.

Lesson: Sufism shows how religion, often co-opted into ego-authoritarianism, can instead teach humility, empathy, and dynamic balance — a spiritual surfing that resists rigid dogma.

Andalusian Spain: A Civilizational Surfboard

Between the 8th and 15th centuries, **Al-Andalus** (Islamic Spain) became a crossroads of cultures: Muslim, Jewish, and Christian scholars translated texts, debated philosophy, and co-created knowledge. It was not utopia — conflicts existed — but it was one of history's most remarkable experiments in **surfing plurality**.

- **Ego (Islamic Rule):** Muslim rulers governed, often asserting dominance.
- **Neutral (Knowledge as Anchor):** Greek philosophy, Indian mathematics, and Persian medicine were translated into Arabic and

Latin. Knowledge was shared across boundaries, becoming a Neutral platform.

- **Opposite (Plural Voices):** Jewish and Christian scholars were included in debates, synagogues and churches coexisted with mosques, and intellectual exchange was institutionalized.

Surfing Example: The philosopher **Averroes (Ibn Rushd)** wrote extensive commentaries on Aristotle, later influencing Thomas Aquinas and shaping European thought. This was not one culture "winning," but a surfing exchange: Ego ambition (Islamic empire) riding Neutral data (Aristotle) and embracing Opposite voices (Jewish translators, Christian philosophers).

Lesson: Andalusian Spain demonstrates that civilizations thrive not by silencing others but by surfing diversity. When cultures welcome Neutral anchors (science, philosophy) and Opposite voices (other faiths, minorities), they unleash a wave of creativity that can transform the world.

Why These Traditions Matter Today

- **Against Religious Ego:** Sufism and Andalusia prove that Islam does not have to mean authoritarian hierarchy. The same tradition that gave us rigid clerical states also produced mysticism, pluralism, and Renaissance sparks.
- **For Surfing Culture:** These traditions embody the central thesis of surfing: **ego checked, facts honored, empathy included.**
- **Modern Implication:** In a world of polarization, citing Sufism and Andalusian Spain reminds us that civilizations already hold the seeds of surfing within their own histories. It is not "foreign" to balance, flow, and humility — it is deeply human.

7.3. The Role of Arts: Surfing Through Story & Imagination

Art has always been the **training ground of surfing culture**. Where politics reduces complexity to slogans, art restores multiplicity.

- **Multi-narrator novels.**
- William Faulkner's *As I Lay Dying* tells one family's story through 15 different voices. No single "truth" dominates; readers must surf the contradictions.
- Contemporary polyphonic novels (like Orhan Pamuk's *Snow*) do similar cultural surfing.
- **Films that humanize enemies.**
- *Letters from Iwo Jima* shows WWII from Japanese soldiers' perspectives.
- The surf: Ego (our patriotic truth) meets Opposite (their humanity), anchored by Neutral history.
- **Theater of the Oppressed (Augusto Boal).**
- Audiences step into roles, swapping positions with actors. They must argue the other side.
- It is empathy as practice, not lecture. A civic surfing rehearsal.
- **Music.**
- Jazz improvisation is pure surfing: Ego (solo), Neutral (rhythm, key), Opposite (other players' riffs).
- Hip-hop battles often mirror this — multiple perspectives contesting, rebalancing, co-creating.

Surfing culture is therefore not just governance; it is *aesthetic practice*. The more societies produce art that multiplies voices and forces perspective-shifting, the more resilient they become against Ego traps.

7.4. Toward a Surfing Culture: Flexibility as Wisdom

Rigid truths comfort us but kill adaptability. Surfing culture, by contrast, elevates:
- **Flexibility over rigidity.** Truth is not static; it is lived in motion.

- **Humility over dogma.** No side owns the full story; Neutral anchors are always provisional.
- **Flow over freeze.** Ego wants control, Neutral wants rules, Empathy wants harmony — surfing honors *flowing balance.*

A surfing culture doesn't abandon truth, but accepts that truth requires constant re-surfacing, re-balancing, re-hearing.

Why it matters now:
- In polarized democracies, only surfing culture can rebuild trust.
- In global governance, only surfing culture can allow diverse civilizations to share rules without domination.
- In everyday life, only surfing culture can allow families, workplaces, and communities to argue without breaking apart.

👉 Surfing wisdom is not "soft." It is survival intelligence in an age of waves: climate change, AI, mass migration, pandemics, nationalism.

8. Training Future Leaders: Surf Academies

8.1. Vision

What if future presidents, CEOs, and teachers trained in **Surf Academies**?

8.2. Curriculum
- **Negotiation Labs:** Practice union vs. management.
- **Empathy Drills:** Argue sincerely as your rival.
- **Fact Anchors:** Validate every policy claim.
- **Crisis Surfing:** Simulated pandemics, wars, climate shocks.

8.3. Certification

Graduates earn **Surfing Competence Badges**, proving they can balance ego, facts, and empathy under pressure.

👉 Surf Academies would transform leadership pipelines worldwide.

9. Exercises for the Future Citizen

- **Surfing Diary for Kids:** Daily journaling of Your–Neutral–Opposite.
- **Community Surf Forums:** Local councils adopt three-position debates.
- **Town Hall Surfing:** Citizens must present all three positions before voting.

👉 Small daily practices build a resilient civic culture.

10. Closing: Toward a Civilization of Surfers

Civilizations collapse when locked in ego (Rome, Soviet Union).
Civilizations stagnate when obsessed with facts alone (bureaucratic empires).
Civilizations dissolve when empathy is unchecked by reality (utopian communes).

The **Surfing Society** offers a way forward:

- **Education** raises surfers.
- **Institutions** stabilize surfers.
- **Media** communicates surfers.
- **Economies** reward surfers.
- **Culture** honors surfers.
- **Leadership Academies** train surfers.

This is not utopia. It is survival. It is the only way to ride the waves of climate, AI, inequality, and war without drowning.

A civilization of surfers will never eliminate storms. But it will know how to ride them — with dignity, truth, and compassion in motion.

Chapter 9: Exercises for the Future Citizen

If surfing governance requires institutions, and surfing culture requires wisdom, then surfing democracy requires something even deeper: **surfing citizens**. No reform endures if people themselves cannot embody the balance of ego, truth, and empathy in their own lives.

The waves of crisis — climate change, polarization, war, inequality — are not abstract. They crash daily into the lives of families, neighborhoods, and workplaces. The question becomes: how do we **train ourselves as everyday surfers**, so that we are ready when the bigger waves come?

This chapter presents **exercises, methods, and stories** to make surfing a habit of ordinary life.

9.1. Surfing Diary: Training the Eye of Balance

A. Why a Surfing Diary?

Just as athletes keep training logs and meditators keep journals, surfers of life need a record. Most of us are trapped in **ego narratives** ("I was right, they were wrong"), or swallowed by empathy fatigue ("I just want everyone happy"), or lost in technocratic numbers ("the facts speak for themselves").

A diary helps us pause and ask: **Where was I standing? Ego, Neutral, or Opposite? Did I surf, or did I sink?**

B. Method: The Three-Column Page

Each day, draw three columns:

1. **Your Position (Ego):** What did I want today? Where did I defend myself, my pride, my needs?
2. **Neutral Position (Facts):** What actually happened? What was measurable, verifiable, external?
3. **Opposite Position (Empathy):** What did the other person/side need? What perspective was excluded?

Then add a **Surfing Reflection:** Could I have shifted positions? What would surfing look like in this moment?

B. Example: Workplace Conflict

- **Ego:** I was furious my colleague dismissed my idea in the meeting.
- **Neutral:** She had limited time and was pressured to finish the agenda.
- **Opposite:** She may have felt my suggestion threatened her project, not me personally.
- **Surfing Reflection:** Next time, I can ask to revisit the idea privately, validating her constraints but keeping my voice present.

☞ Over time, the diary **re-trains the mind**: instead of reflexive ego reactions, we learn to see three perspectives at once.

9.2. Community Surf Forums: Democracy in Miniature

A. Why Local Surfing?

National polarization feels impossible to fix, but local forums show that ordinary people can surf when given the tools.

B Model: The Three-Seat Debate

- Each local council or school board sets up **three chairs**:
- **Your Position seat**: A citizen speaks from their own interest.
- **Neutral seat**: A citizen presents data, expert evidence.
- **Opposite seat**: A citizen argues from the viewpoint of the least heard.

Before any vote, each seat must be filled and voiced.

C. Case: Irish Citizen Assemblies

When Ireland faced divisive issues (abortion, marriage equality), it didn't rely on politicians alone. Randomly selected citizens listened to experts (Neutral), voiced personal convictions (Ego), and heard testimonies from affected groups (Opposite). The result: surprising consensus and legitimacy.

☞ Community forums that adopt three-seat surfing become **micro-democracies** — antidotes to polarization.

9.3. Town Hall Surfing: Ritualized Perspective-Shifting

Imagine a new rule: **Before any vote, a citizen must articulate all three positions.**

A. Process

At town hall meetings or even school board gatherings:

- Each participant is required to **state the Ego case, the Neutral facts, and the Opposite empathy** before casting a ballot.
- This ritual slows decision-making but ensures that empathy and truth enter the bloodstream of democracy.

B Example: Local Housing Dispute

- **Ego (homeowners):** We fear losing property value if apartments are built.
- **Neutral:** Data shows housing shortage, rising rents, traffic patterns.
- **Opposite (renters & homeless):** Families are priced out, youth cannot stay.

When citizens rehearse this structure, decisions gain legitimacy even when unpopular.

9.4. Family Surfing: Marriage, Parenting, and Everyday Peace

Surfing is not only for parliaments. Families are the most constant waves we ride.

A. Marriage Surfing

Most marital conflicts repeat the same pattern:

- Ego: "You never listen to me."

- Neutral: "This week you worked 60 hours and we spoke only 2 evenings."
- Opposite: "Your partner feels invisible, not unloved."

Surfing in marriage means pausing: *What's my ego? What's the fact? What's their hidden need?* Couples who journal or role-play these positions can transform fights into growth.

B. Parenting Surfing

Children live in Ego: "I want candy now!" Parents often reply with Neutral: "Sugar isn't healthy." Surfing requires adding Opposite: "You feel left out because others got candy."

By acknowledging all three, parents teach balance, not just obedience.

C. Case Study: Family Surfing Ritual

One family instituted "Surfing Sundays": before dinner, each member shared:
- Their biggest Ego wish that week.
- One Neutral fact they learned.
- One Opposite perspective they tried to imagine.

Result: empathy and humility became family habits.

9.5. Digital Surfing: Social Media Detox for Citizens

The digital world is designed to trap us in Ego (likes, outrage) or Empathy manipulation (viral sob stories without context). Neutral facts drown.

Exercises

- **Surf the Feed:** For every post you react to, ask: *Whose Ego does this serve? What Neutral evidence exists? Who is the Opposite voice?*
- **Opposite Follow:** Deliberately follow at least one credible source you disagree with, not to convert but to **surf perspectives**.
- **Neutral Anchor Alerts:** Use fact-check sites and independent aggregators to reset your feed.

 Surfing citizens don't abandon digital life — they reclaim it.

9.6. Exercises for Civic Surfing: Training Like Athletes

1. **Role-Reversal Debates:** In community clubs or schools, assign students to argue the side they oppose.
2. **Fact Anchoring Games:** Teams compete to find neutral evidence fastest — with sources ranked by reliability.
3. **Empathy Walks:** Volunteers spend a day in the shoes of the "Opposite" — shadowing a worker, immigrant, or person with disability — then share in forums.

☞ Surfing is a muscle. It grows only with practice.

9.7. The Long View: Citizens as Wave-Riders of Civilization

History shows:

- Civilizations collapsed when citizens froze in Ego (Rome's elite decadence, Nazi Germany).
- Civilizations stagnated when citizens froze in Neutral bureaucracy (late Qing China, Soviet Union).
- Civilizations dissolved when citizens drowned in utopian empathy (19th-century communes).

The only societies that endured were those where **citizens learned to surf**:
- Athens in its democratic experiments.
- Renaissance Florence balancing bankers, artists, and guilds.
- Nordic countries today, where civic trust allows surfing between markets, welfare, and globalism.

9.8. Conclusion: Surfing as Daily Citizenship

Surfing is not just for presidents or CEOs. It begins at the breakfast table, the school debate, the neighborhood council, the workplace team, and the phone in our hands.

The daily practice of surfing — diaries, forums, town halls, family rituals, digital detox, role-reversal exercises — creates **habits of balance** that no demagogue can easily break.

The future citizen is not passive.

They are a surfer: aware of ego, anchored in facts, open to the opposite.
They know storms will come, but they ride them with dignity.

□ Surfing Citizen Checklist
Daily Practices for Balance & Democracy

□ Surfing Diary

Daily 3-column journaling: Ego, Neutral, Opposite + reflection.

□ Community Surf Forums

Three-seat debates in councils: Ego, Facts, Empathy before decisions.

□ Town Hall Surfing

Citizens must articulate all three positions before voting.

□□□ Family Surfing

Marriage & parenting with Ego-Neutral-Opposite dialogue rituals.

□ Digital Surfing

Check feeds: Whose Ego? What Facts? Which Opposite voices missing?

□ Role-Reversal & Empathy Drills

Practice debates, fact hunts, and empathy walks.

Surfing Citizen Checklist Diagram □ — a one-page visual toolkit for daily practice:

1.   □ **Surfing Diary** → Daily 3-column journaling: Ego, Neutral, Opposite + reflection.
2.   □ **Community Surf Forums** → Three-seat debates: Ego, Facts, Empathy before decisions.
3.   □ **Town Hall Surfing** → Citizens must articulate all three positions before voting.
4.   □ **Family Surfing** → Marriage & parenting with Ego–Neutral–Opposite rituals.
5.   □ **Digital Surfing** → Ask of each feed: Whose Ego? What Facts? Which Opposite missing?

6. 🎭 **Role-Reversal & Empathy Drills** → Practice debates, fact hunts, and empathy walks.

👉 This works as a **practical appendix** to Chapter 9 — can print it, pin it at home, or use it in classrooms, forums, or workshops.

Chapter 10 – The Wisdom of the Opposite: Common Ground as the Seed of Peace

1. Why Common Ground Matters

Every conflict begins with **two positions locked against each other**. A spouse insists on being right, a manager refuses to budge on terms, a political leader rejects compromise. Each side, convinced of its own righteousness, digs deeper into the trench of self-justification.

But history shows: **conflicts end only when common ground is found**.

- Families heal when both parents realize they love the same child, even if they disagree on methods.
- Businesses grow when managers and workers both agree that survival of the company benefits all.
- Nations transform when rival groups recognize that their deepest fear — chaos, collapse, or violence — is the same.

Common ground is not a soft illusion. It is the **hard foundation of peace and transformation**. The paradox is: it often lies hidden in the opposite position. To find it, one must step outside one's own ego, and into the shoes of the other.

2. Forgiveness vs. First Consideration

Forgiveness is a beautiful act — but it often comes too late. Forgiveness is **after the damage**, after years of bitterness, after relationships are scarred.

First consideration is wiser. It asks: *What if I thought of the other side first?* Not to surrender, but to foresee.

- In a family quarrel: instead of screaming, a parent pauses — "My child is angry, but what does he really need?"
- In a business negotiation: instead of pushing profit, an entrepreneur asks — "If I were my client, what would I demand?"
- In politics: instead of demonizing the opposition, leaders ask — "What fear is driving them to resist?"

This practice **saves years of pain**. It doesn't wait for forgiveness; it prevents the wound. It is the essence of wisdom.

3. The Danger of Misinterpretation ⚠

Here lies a trap. Ancient wisdom — especially Buddhist philosophy — warns: *anger burns the vessel that holds it*. This insight is psychologically true: anger consumes the one who clings to it.

But misused, it becomes dangerous. Some interpret it as:

- "Be endlessly tolerant."
- "Always forgive."
- "Never resist."

This mistake leads to:

- Spouses enduring abuse.
- Workers accepting exploitation.
- Citizens allowing dictators to dominate.

That is not wisdom. That is submission.

Wisdom calms anger — but does not silence your rights.

4. The Balanced Way

The **Three Positions** prevent misinterpretation:

- **Your Position** = voice your truth, protect your dignity. Without this, you vanish.
- **Neutral Position** = anchor yourself in facts, evidence, fairness.
- **Opposite Position** = step into the other side's shoes — not to surrender, but to see deeper truths and hidden fears.

When you **surf among all three**, you discover common ground without abandoning self-respect. You move toward peace with clarity, not passivity.

5. Case Studies

Toyota Lean Production

In post-war Japan, workers felt used and voiceless. Management feared strikes would ruin recovery. Instead of crushing opposition, Toyota invited workers to improve production lines. Workers voiced grievances, managers listened, and the system of *Kaizen* was born — small continuous improvements. The result: efficiency for the company, dignity for the workers. **Common ground created global leadership.**

Taiwan's Democratic Transformation

In the 1980s, Taiwan faced authoritarian rigidity. Opposition demanded freedom; the ruling party feared chaos. Instead of waiting for civil war, Taiwan's leaders integrated opposition voices **before violence exploded** — legalizing parties, reforming institutions, strengthening neutral courts. The result: one of Asia's most peaceful transitions to democracy. **Common ground stabilized freedom.**

Nelson Mandela

After 27 years in prison, Mandela emerged with every right to remain angry. But he realized: holding anger would burn South Africa itself. Yet he did not surrender rights. He fought for elections, for equal dignity, for institutions. He forgave personally, but built systems of justice. **Common ground was created through forgiveness with strength.**

6. Practices for Safe Wisdom

1. **The First Opposition Habit**
   - In every discussion, invite the opposition voice *first*.
   - Listen before defending.
2. **The Anchor Rights Rule**
   - Write down your non-negotiables before dialogue: dignity, fairness, truth.
   - Never cross them, no matter how sympathetic you feel.
3. **The One Agreement + One Boundary Exercise**
   - Always acknowledge one valid point from the other side.
   - Always state one clear line you cannot cross.
4. **Family Reflection Practice**

- When upset with spouse/child, write: "If I were them, what would I need?"
- Then write: "What is my line that must be respected?"

5. **Business Application Drill**
- Before negotiation, role-play as client or competitor.
- Identify what would make them say "yes" without betraying your value.

7. From Conflict to Peace with Dignity

Peace is not silence. Harmony is not submission.

True wisdom is calming anger so that you can **act wisely, fight smarter, negotiate stronger, and transform deeper**.

- Families thrive when rights and love balance.
- Businesses grow when dignity and profit align.
- Societies flourish when democracy respects opposition while protecting freedoms.

The final insight:

Common ground is the seed of peace — but only when it grows in soil where rights are protected, dignity is preserved, and awakening comes from within, not from forced obedience.

Chapter 11 – Calming Anger Without Losing Rights

1. The Fire of Anger: Buddhist Insight

For thousands of years, Buddhist psychology has taught that anger is like a burning coal held in the hand: the first one it injures is the one who grasps it. This metaphor, repeated in many sutras, expresses a deep truth: **anger consumes the vessel that holds it.**

Modern psychology confirms this insight:

- Chronic anger raises cortisol and blood pressure.
- It weakens the immune system, shortens life expectancy.
- Anger-driven decisions often escalate conflict rather than resolve it.

The wisdom here is profound: unchecked anger poisons not only societies but the self.

Yet the insight carries danger. Stripped of context, "anger burns the vessel" is too often misused to justify **submission**. People in abusive marriages, workers under exploitation, or citizens under dictatorships are told: *"Let go of anger. Forgive. Be silent."*

This is not wisdom. It is manipulation.

2. The Danger of Misinterpretation: Sympathy vs. Submission

Anger, like all emotions, carries energy. To deny it entirely is to deny part of human dignity. Across cultures, those in power have used "forgiveness" rhetoric to disarm the oppressed:

- **Domestic abuse:** Victims told to endure "for the family."
- **Workplace exploitation:** Employees urged to be "team players," suppressing resentment while management profits.
- **Dictatorships:** Citizens reminded that "resistance brings chaos," so submission is framed as virtue.

This is sympathy weaponized into silence. It transforms the noble impulse to forgive into a demand that the weak accept damage without resistance.

☞ True wisdom does not call for endless tolerance. It calls for **balance**: calm the destructive flame of rage without extinguishing the fire of dignity.

3. The Balanced Way: Anger as Compass, Not Master

How, then, do we surf anger without drowning in it or denying it?

A. Three Positions Applied to Anger

1. **Your Position (Ego):**
   - Acknowledge the wound, the injustice.
   - "I am hurt. I am disrespected. This is not acceptable."
   - Without this voice, you vanish into submission.
2. **Neutral Position (Facts):**
   - Anchor the feeling with data: What exactly happened? Who said what? What law was broken?
   - Anger without facts becomes paranoia. Anchored, it becomes evidence for justice.
3. **Opposite Position (Empathy):**
   - Ask: What fear, need, or blindness drives the other side?
   - This does not excuse harm. It explains context, which makes strategy sharper.

Surfing anger means cycling between all three: self-protection, evidence, and perspective.

B. Anger vs. Violence

- **Anger as Master:** leads to violence, destruction, cycles of revenge.
- **Anger as Compass:** points to injustice, but strategy decides the path.

Mandela after prison is the archetype: he acknowledged his anger, but he refused to let it master him. He surfed it into strategy, turning fury into clarity.

C. Peace With Justice, Not Peace By Silence

- **Peace by Silence:** the graveyard of rights. It ends conflict by suffocating voices.
- **Peace with Justice:** anger calmed enough to dialogue, but dignity uncompromised.

This is the balanced way: calm emotions while protecting rights.

4. Case Studies: Anger Surfed Into Transformation

1. The U.S. Civil Rights Movement

- **Ego (Your Position):** Black citizens enraged by Jim Crow, lynchings, humiliation.
- **Neutral:** Data on segregation, income inequality, court rulings.
- **Opposite:** Even appealing to white conscience — "If one group is chained, the whole society is chained."
- **Surfing Outcome:** Leaders like Martin Luther King Jr. transformed anger into disciplined nonviolence, producing legal change.

2. Poland's Solidarity Movement

- Workers furious at exploitation in Gdańsk shipyards.
- Anger was channeled through **Neutral anchors**: economic data, human rights principles.
- By reaching out to **Opposite perspectives** (Catholic Church, intellectuals, even reformists within the regime), the movement found common ground.
- Result: The largest peaceful democratic transition in Eastern Europe.

3. #MeToo Movement

- **Ego:** Millions of women released decades of anger at harassment.
- **Neutral:** Systematic data, court cases, testimonies.
- **Opposite:** Even men were invited to see the fear their silence enabled.
- Surfing anger created not just personal healing but legal reforms and cultural shifts.

5. Practices: Calming Without Submission

Here are **practical exercises** for families, workplaces, and citizens:

1. **The Anger Journal**

   - Step 1: Write down what made you furious.
   - Step 2: Separate facts from interpretations.
   - Step 3: Write one sentence imagining the other side's fear.
   - Step 4: Decide on an action that preserves dignity without escalation.

2. **The Anchor Rights Rule**
   - Before any negotiation or dialogue, write 3 non-negotiables: dignity, fairness, truth.
   - These are your "surfboard." Anger may rock you, but you won't drown.

3. **The One Agreement + One Boundary Drill**
   - In conflict, always state:
   - One valid point from the other side (agreement).
   - One clear line they must not cross (boundary).

4. **Family Surfing Reflection**
   - When upset, ask: *If I were my spouse/child, what would I need?*
   - Then ask: *What boundary must they respect for me to stay whole?*

5. **Business Application**
   - Before entering negotiation, role-play as client, worker, or regulator.
   - Ask: *What would make them say yes without making me betray my value?*

5. Cultural & Philosophical Anchors

- **Buddhism:** Anger burns the self first. True — but never confuse this with accepting injustice.

- **Stoicism:** Anger is passion ungoverned by reason; dignity comes from choosing rational response.
- **Ubuntu:** "I am because we are." My anger matters, but so does the community's healing.
- **Daoism:** Flow with the wave — resist too rigidly, and you snap; ride flexibly, and you redirect force.

Together they show: calming anger is not submission but transformation into clarity.

7. Global Implications: Surfing Collective Anger

The 21st century is full of angry societies:

- Farmers in India protesting unfair laws.
- Citizens in Hong Kong demanding freedom.
- Americans divided by race, inequality, and politics.
- Youth worldwide furious at climate inaction.

Each wave of anger carries danger — but also possibility. If anger is surfed through the Three Positions, it becomes **the energy of transformation**. If denied or weaponized, it becomes chaos or authoritarianism.

9. Family Cases: Anger in the Home

Case 1: Parenting in Conflict

A teenage son shouts: *"You never understand me!"* The father, furious, raises his voice: *"Don't speak to me like that!"* Ego collides with Ego.
- **Your Position (Ego):** Parent wants respect. Child wants independence.
- **Neutral (Facts):** Son has been studying late, missing family dinners. Father is stressed from work. Both are exhausted.
- **Opposite (Empathy):** The son feels invisible, craving recognition. The father feels disrespected, craving gratitude.

Surfing Outcome:

Instead of escalating, the father pauses: *"If I were you, I'd feel suffocated. But as your father, I also need respect. Let's set a time to talk tomorrow calmly."*
Anger is calmed, dignity is preserved. The child learns conflict without rupture.

Case 2: Marriage Argument

A wife discovers her husband made a large purchase without consulting her. She explodes: *"You never think of us!"* He fires back: *"It's my money too!"*
- **Your Position (Ego):** Wife demands shared decision-making. Husband defends autonomy.
- **Neutral (Facts):** Bank account shows funds stretched thin.
- **Opposite (Empathy):** Wife fears instability. Husband feels controlled.

Surfing Outcome:

Instead of silent bitterness or endless screaming, they adopt the **One Agreement + One Boundary Drill**:

- Agreement: "Yes, you contribute income, and you deserve freedom."
- Boundary: "But purchases over $1,000 must be discussed first."

Peace without silence. Conflict becomes a new rule of dignity.

10. Workplace Cases: Anger in Teams

Case 1: Employee vs. Manager

An employee is furious after being excluded from a major project. She storms into the manager's office: *"You always overlook me!"*
- **Ego:** Employee wants recognition. Manager wants efficiency.
- **Neutral:** The project had tight deadlines; fewer people reduced complexity.
- **Opposite:** Employee feels undervalued. Manager fears too many voices would slow progress.

Surfing Outcome:

The manager says: *"I see you're frustrated, and I admit you've contributed well. The fact is, I had to decide quickly. Let's plan how you can lead the next project."*
Anger is acknowledged, facts clarified, dignity preserved.

Case 2: Union vs. Company

Workers strike for higher pay. Management insists: "We can't afford it."

- **Ego (Workers):** Demand higher wages.
- **Ego (Company):** Protect profit margins.
- **Neutral:** Financial audits show rising profits, but automation costs are looming.
- **Opposite:** Workers fear poverty; managers fear collapse.

Surfing Outcome:

Through negotiation, both sides agree on **profit-sharing bonuses**: when the company does well, workers benefit. Anger is redirected into partnership.

11. Business Cases: Surfing in Negotiation

Case 1: Client Relations

A supplier delivers late. The client rages: *"You're ruining my business!"*
- **Ego (Client):** Feels betrayed, reputation at stake.
- **Neutral:** Shipment delayed due to customs inspection.
- **Opposite:** Supplier also losing money, under stress.

Surfing Outcome:

The supplier calms the client's anger: *"I understand you're furious — if I were you, I'd be too. The facts are customs delayed us. To protect your business, we'll ship by air next time at our cost."*
Dignity on both sides remains. Anger becomes trust.

Case 2: International Trade Disputes

A U.S. company accuses its Asian partner of cheating on contracts. Lawsuits loom.

- **Ego:** U.S. side demands accountability. Asian side defends honor.
- **Neutral:** Documents show ambiguous clauses.
- **Opposite:** U.S. fears reputational loss; Asian side fears loss of face.

Surfing Outcome:

Instead of a destructive lawsuit, mediators create a new contract with clearer clauses + shared oversight board.
Result: Partnership survives. Anger redirected into stronger systems.

12. Lessons Across Contexts

1. **In Families:** Anger is often love in disguise — protect dignity, but listen for fear.
2. **In Workplaces:** Anger signals exclusion or disrespect — facts + empathy transform it into productivity.
3. **In Business:** Anger usually masks fear of loss — surf by naming the fear, clarifying facts, and offering dignity.

13. Final Insight: The Flame That Guides

Anger is not always a fire to extinguish. It is also a torch — pointing to injustice, unmet needs, or broken systems. The challenge is not to let the flame burn uncontrolled, nor to smother it in silence.

☞ The art is to surf it:

- Calm the fire.
- Protect your rights.
- Transform it into clarity.

This is how families grow stronger, workplaces become fairer, businesses more resilient, and societies more just.

The Anger Surfboard

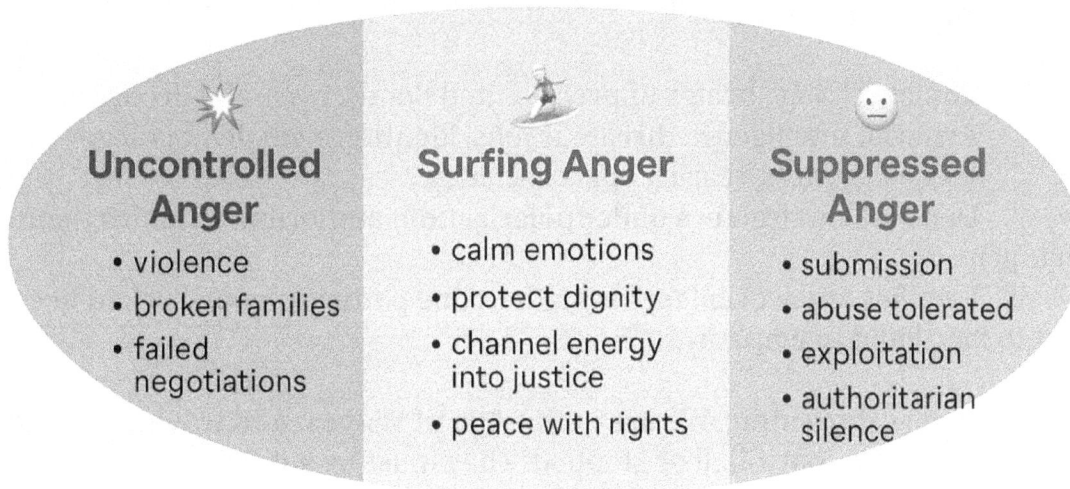

Uncontrolled Anger	Surfing Anger	Suppressed Anger
• violence • broken families • failed negotiations	• calm emotions • protect dignity • channel energy into justice • peace with rights	• submission • abuse tolerated • exploitation • authoritarian silence

This visual anchors Chapter 11: it shows clearly that anger is not to be destroyed or silenced, but surfed into clarity and transformation.

Anger Surfboard Diagram:

- **Uncontrolled Anger** → Violence, broken families, failed negotiations, collapsed revolutions.
- **Suppressed Anger** → Submission, abuse tolerated, exploitation, authoritarian silence.
- **Surfing Anger** → Calm emotions, protect dignity, channel energy into justice, peace with rights.

This visual anchors Chapter 11: it shows clearly that anger is not to be destroyed or silenced, but surfed into clarity and transformation.

Chapter 12 – Surfing Civilization: The Manifesto for a Balanced Future

1. The Age of Storms

Humanity stands at a crossroads.

- Climate change brings unprecedented floods, fires, and droughts.
- Artificial intelligence threatens jobs, identity, even democracy.
- Inequality rises, tearing apart societies.
- Democracies fracture under polarization; authoritarian states tighten their grip.
- Families and workplaces echo the same pattern: people locked in ego, deaf to fact, blind to empathy.

We are not in calm waters. We are in **the Age of Waves**. And waves, by their nature, cannot be controlled or stopped. They must be **surfed**.

2. Why Old Models Fail

History has shown us three dead ends:

1. **Ego Civilizations**
   - Ancient empires obsessed with conquest (Rome's decadence, fascism's rage).
   - They collapsed under their own arrogance.

2. **Neutral Bureaucracies**
   - Societies worshipping systems, numbers, control (Qing Dynasty's ossified exams, Soviet technocracy).
   - They stagnated, losing creativity and humanity.

3. **Empathy Utopias**
   - Movements that gave everything to "the people" without anchors (utopian communes, Venezuela's populism).
   - They dissolved in chaos, unable to sustain themselves.

☞ The future cannot repeat these traps. Only **surfing — the dynamic balance of ego, fact, and empathy — offers survival.**

3. The Surfer Citizen

Every transformation begins with individuals. The surfer citizen practices daily balance:

- In family disputes: voices self-respect, checks facts, imagines the other's need.
- In workplaces: negotiates wages by combining ego, profit data, and empathy for management pressures.
- In democracy: reads news critically, separating outrage from fact and empathy.
- Online: resists echo chambers, follows opposite views, seeks neutral evidence.

The surfer citizen is not passive. They are awake, resilient, and adaptable.

4. The Surfer Family

Surfing begins at the most intimate level.

- **Parenting:** Not domination, not indulgence, but balance. A parent listens (opposite), anchors rules in fairness (neutral), yet protects authority (ego).
- **Marriage:** Not silencing anger, not endless battles. Couples surf by stating agreements + boundaries, turning fights into growth.
- **Generations:** Elders provide Neutral anchors of history, youth provide Ego energy, and both learn empathy across the divide.

A surfing family does not avoid storms. It learns to ride them together.

5. The Surfer Workplace & Business

Businesses that cling only to ego (profit) will collapse under social backlash. Those that worship technocracy (efficiency) will lose soul. Those that give everything away (empathy populism) will burn resources.

Future companies must **surf**:
- **Ego:** Innovate, compete, pursue excellence.
- **Neutral:** Transparent facts, ESG data, sustainability metrics.
- **Opposite:** Workers' dignity, community welfare, environmental voices.

Case Studies:

- *Patagonia*: Anchors profit in Neutral sustainability, Opposite respect for nature, Ego in product excellence.
- *Mondragon*: Worker-owned cooperative balancing profit, democracy, and solidarity.
- *Novo Nordisk*: Balances pharmaceutical profit, health data, and empathy for patients.

☞ The surfer corporation thrives because it rides three waves at once.

6. The Surfer Democracy

Democracy is in crisis worldwide. Polarization turns every election into civil war.

But surfing provides a way forward:

- **Ego (Your Position):** Local constituencies must be represented.
- **Neutral (Facts):** Independent courts and science councils anchor truth.
- **Opposite (Empathy):** Minorities and vulnerable groups must be protected by law.

Institutional Surfing Tools:

- Citizen assemblies (Ireland).
- Truth & Reconciliation commissions (South Africa).
- Parliamentary debates requiring all three positions before votes.

☞ Democracies that fail to surf collapse into tribalism. Democracies that learn to surf endure.

7. The Surfer Economy

Capitalism must be civilized, not abandoned.

- **Trap 1: Ego Capitalism:** Exploit workers, destroy planet.
- **Trap 2: Neutral Technocracy:** GDP obsession, ignoring dignity.
- **Trap 3: Empathy Populism:** Give to all, collapse in hyperinflation.

Surfing Economies Work:

- *Germany's Social Market Model*: Free markets + worker protections.
- *Nordic Countries*: High innovation, high taxes, high trust.
- *UBI Experiments (Finland, Kenya)*: Dignity increased without laziness.

Surfing capitalism means: profit, sustainability, and human dignity in one flow.

8. The Surfer Culture & Philosophy

Culture must shift from rigid dogma to surfing wisdom.

- **Ego Cultures:** Hierarchies, nationalism, blind obedience.
- **Neutral Cultures:** Bureaucracy, lifeless systems.
- **Empathy Cultures:** Romantic idealism, unsustainable utopias.

Surfing wisdom honors **flow over rigidity**:

- Buddhism's Middle Way.
- Stoicism's discipline.
- Ubuntu's "I am because we are."
- Daoism's water-like adaptability.

Art, literature, and film can rehearse surfing:

- Multi-narrator novels (Faulkner).
- Enemy-humanizing films (*Letters from Iwo Jima*).
- Participatory theater (Augusto Boal).

Culture becomes the training ground of surfers.

9. The Surfer Civilization

What would a *civilization of surfers* look like?

- **Education:** Surf Academies teaching every child perspective-switching, empathy drills, fact anchoring.
- **Democracy:** Laws requiring three-perspective debates before decisions.
- **Media:** Stories labeled Ego, Neutral, Opposite.
- **Economy:** Firms required to disclose triple-impact reports: profit, environment, human dignity.
- **Global Governance:** Surf Councils institutionalizing Neutral science, Opposite testimonies, and Ego interests in climate, trade, and war.

10 Lessons From History

- **Rome** collapsed in Ego arrogance.
- **Qing China** stagnated in Neutral bureaucracy.
- **Utopian communes** dissolved in unchecked Empathy.

But societies that surf — Athens in democracy, Renaissance Florence balancing guilds, Nordic countries balancing capitalism and welfare — thrived.

11. Final Manifesto: Ride the Wave

We are surfers, whether we know it or not. The waves are already here: climate, AI, pandemics, war, inequality. The choice is not whether to surf, but whether to surf **well**.

- Families survive when they surf anger into dialogue.
- Workplaces thrive when they surf conflict into productivity.
- Businesses endure when they surf profit, sustainability, and dignity together.
- Democracies flourish when they surf ego, facts, and empathy in institutions.
- Civilizations endure when they surf waves instead of drowning in them.

☞ The civilization of surfers is not utopia. It is **survival with dignity**. It is not submission, nor domination. It is wisdom in motion.

The wave is coming.
Grab your board.
Learn to surf.

Surfing Civilization Diagram
Riding Waves Instead of Drowning in Them

Ego Civilization
(Domination, Arrogance)

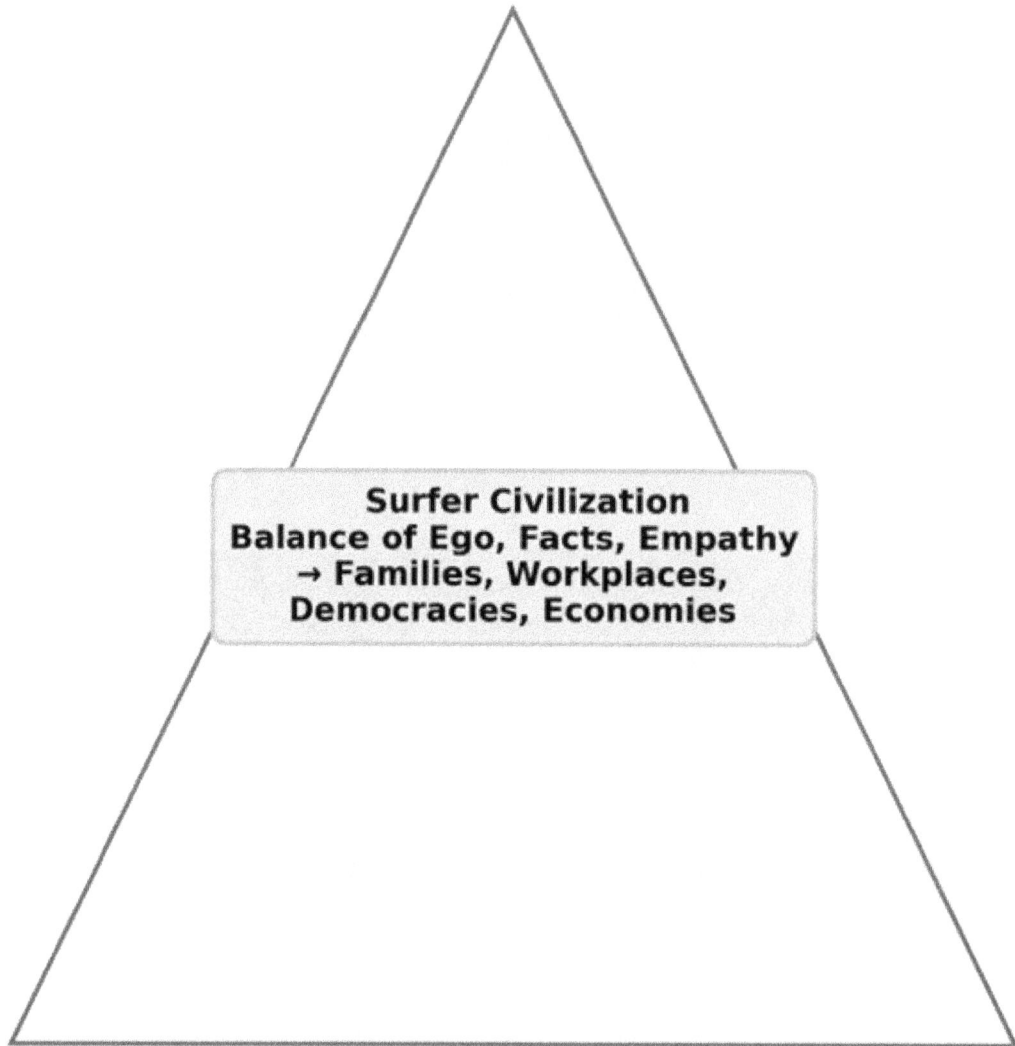

Surfer Civilization
Balance of Ego, Facts, Empathy
→ Families, Workplaces,
Democracies, Economies

Neutral Bureaucracy
(Stagnation, Technocracy)

Empathy Utopias
(Collapse, Chaos)

🌐 **Surfing Civilization Diagram**

- **Ego Civilization (Domination, Arrogance)** → collapses under its own pride.

- **Neutral Bureaucracy (Stagnation, Technocracy)** → ossifies into lifeless systems.
- **Empathy Utopias (Collapse, Chaos)** → dissolve without anchors.
- 🏄 **Surfer Civilization (Center, Gold Zone)** → balancing Ego, Facts, and Empathy across families, workplaces, democracies, and economies.

👉 a **civilization that rides the waves instead of drowning in them**.

Afterword

Through many years of life and work, I have inevitably encountered countless moments of disappointment, shock, and sorrow. The most painful experiences, however, have often come not from distant adversaries but from those closest to me—people I once considered friends, even best friends.

Chinese culture, with its intricate and tangled layers, is like a rope woven from a thousand different strands. Its strength lies in resilience, but its weakness is that everyone can always find an excuse within it—to escape, to evade, or even to harm. Family ties, when mishandled, so easily turn to enmity; business partnerships collapse into lawsuits with alarming frequency. In the face of such wounds, apart from forgetting, there often seems to be no remedy.

Yet one morning, I suddenly realized that perhaps there is a simpler way. By placing each conflict into **three different positions** for examination, the situation begins to change. From *my own position*, to the *neutral position*, and finally to the *opposite position*, space opens up between reactions. What once felt like a dead end can loosen; what once felt unbearable may find a path forward.

From this realization, after finishing my daily work, I sketched the outline of this book. The metaphor of **surfing** then arose naturally: moving between the three positions like a surfer balancing on the waves—never rigid, never drowning, but always adjusting and moving forward.

This, perhaps, is an unexpected gift from life itself. My hope is that this book can also serve as such a gift to you: a kind of surfboard, helping you find balance and direction in the waves of conflict and uncertainty.

— **ButterflyMan**

www.ingramcontent.com/pod-product-compliance
Lightning Source LLC
LaVergne TN
LVHW061248060426

835508LV00018B/1545